Adventure & Appliqué

Traveling
the World with
Award-Winning
Quilter
Suzanne Marshall

American Quilter's Society
P. O. Box 3290 • Paducah, KY 42002-3290
www.AmericanQuilter.com

Located in Paducah, Kentucky, the American Quilter's Society (AQS) is dedicated to promoting the accomplishments of today's quilters. Through its publications and events, AQS strives to honor today's quiltmakers and their work and to inspire future creativity and innovation in quiltmaking.

Executive Editor: NICOLE C. CHAMBERS
Illustrations: ELAINE WILSON AND LYNDA SMITH
Cover Design: MICHAEL BUCKINGHAM
Quilt Photography: CHARLES R. LYNCH
How-to and Travel Photography: SUZANNE & GARLAND MARSHALL, UNLESS OTHERWISE INDICATED
Maps © 2008 Jupiterimages Corporation

American Quilter's Society
P. O. Box 3290 • Paducah, KY 42002-3290
www.AmericanQuilter.com

Additional copies of this book may be ordered from the American Quilter's Society, PO Box 3290, Paducah, KY 42002-3290, or online at www.AmericanQuilter.com.

Library of Congress Cataloging-in-Publication Data
Marshall, Suzanne
    Adventure & appliqué: traveling the world with award-winning quilter Suzanne Marshall / by Suzanne Marshall.
        p. cm.
    Includes bibliographical references and index.
    Summary: "Learn Marshall's "take-away" appliqué technique. Includes patterns from author's prizewinning quilts. Read comments from judges, both positive and negative"--Provided by publisher.
    ISBN 978-1-57432-947-6 (alk. paper)
    1. Appliqué--Patterns. 2. Quilting--Patterns. I. Title. II. Title: Adventure and appliqué.
    TT779.M284 2008
    746.44'5041--dc22
                    2007052805

Proudly printed and bound in the United States of America

Thanks to Garland, who wrote his comments in my book and has always been supportive and appreciative of my quilting.

This book is dedicated to our grandchildren—

FRONT ROW LEFT TO RIGHT
Sophie, Gracie, Lucy

BACK ROW LEFT TO RIGHT
Jacob, Sasha, Hannah, Elisabeth, Abigail, Meredith
May your lives be filled with adventure.

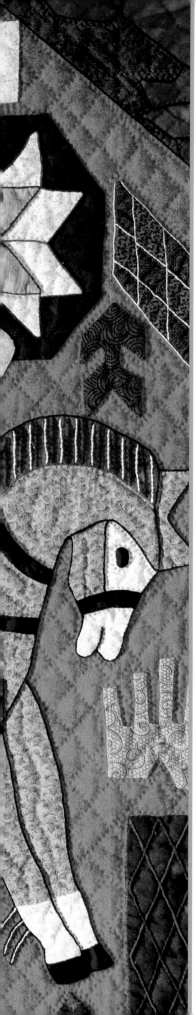

Table of Contents

Foreword by Ricky Tims

If there are silver linings in clouds, I'm confident that Suzanne Marshall stitched them. If there is light at the end of the tunnel, it will come from Suzanne's never-ending encouragement. If anyone ever makes a perfect quilt, I'm placing my bets with Suzanne Marshall.

In 1991, as a fledgling quilter, I attended my first quilt show. It was held at the library in University City, Missouri, a suburb of St. Louis. Suzanne Marshall's quilt CASS GILBERT REMEMBERED won the Best of Show. I was in awe. I had no idea that such amazingly beautiful and perfect creations could be made by humans—that is, if Suzanne Marshall is indeed human. I have found her to be more like an angel sent from heaven—always encouraging me and helping me find my way. She is forever singing the praises of others and quietly blending into a crowd, never vying to be the center of anyone's attention. She is not shy or retiring, quite the contrary. She is enthusiastic, energetic, and a great conversationalist. It is just that she would rather her quilts steal the show—and steal the show they do!

The Encouraging Suzanne Marshall

I had been quilting less than six months when I met Suzanne. She invited me over, or maybe I invited myself, but nevertheless, I took my first few quilt projects over for her critique and review. She all but did cartwheels over everything I showed her, including my first quilt, a sampler with few seams that matched, poor color choices, a bed sheet for backing, and stabbed-stitched/hand quilted with maybe six stitches to the inch. I showed her my small original fabric expressions and she was enthusiastic and complimentary, supportive and encouraging.

She then led me to a spare room to show me her quilts, peeling them like onionskins, one after the other from atop a spare bed. It was like a ballet where each quilt danced solo before wafting off stage to allow the spotlight to shine on another. With each successive unveiling I became more stunned—more in awe. The stories behind each quilt were thoughtful and thought provoking. The stitching was perfection.

Looking back on that day sixteen years ago, I realize how lucky I was and still am. I didn't go away feeling inadequate in the presence of greatness. Rather, I went away feeling inspired, like I had a new world of quilting before me, and the sky was the limit. What a surprise! What a treasure! What a gift Suzanne Marshall gave me! And not just to me, but also to anyone who knows her or has studied under her. She is the consummate cheerleader. She embodies the word encouragement.

The Persistent Suzanne Marshall

Artists are often defined by a body of work. Suzanne has a broad body of work that is made one stitch at a time—by hand. A small quilt might take her a year to create and larger works take much longer. She stitches every day. She takes her projects on trips. She is never idle.

I once heard someone say, "I don't quilt. I wouldn't have the patience for it." Suzanne responded with something I've never forgotten, "It doesn't take patience to do something you love to do." She must love it a lot, because she could not possibly create the number of quilts that she has without having the passion to do so.

Antique textiles dating back hundreds of years have inspired many of her quilts. Traveling with her husband, Garland, she has been able to research her projects by scheduling appointments with curators of museums all over the world. She has had the privilege to examine firsthand many textile pieces that remain permanently in storage and out of sight of the public. It is always a thrill to hear her tell of a new discovery or a visit with a museum curator.

Suzanne Marshall → The Survivor

Shortly before I met Suzanne, she had won a battle with breast cancer. Soon thereafter she began work on an original designed quilt inspired by her experiences. Her MASTECTOMY QUILT opened the door for her to share her experience, which has subsequently resulted in untold numbers of women finding the courage to seek testing.

More recently, Suzanne was in a small airplane over New Guinea. The plane suddenly experienced mechanical problems. Because they were flying over the thick mountainous jungle, there was no place to land. Finally spotting a "landing strip," the pilot landed. The dramatic story is contained in this book, so I'll not spoil it for you now. However, you will come to learn another reason why I call Suzanne Marshall a survivor.

Through Suzanne's stories and quilts, you'll no doubt come to know her: her life, her loves, and her quilts. You will learn that she is an amazing woman and you will come to understand why I love her.

Ricky

The Adventure Begins...

Quilting for me began in the mid-seventies when our four young children needed covers on their beds. Having made clothes for many years, I had accumulated fabric scraps and thought that it would be fun to try making quilts for them. At that time I didn't know anyone who made quilts, so I went to the public library and checked out a book to get started.

My first quilts were patchwork—scrappy and with the patches painstakingly cut out one at a time by drawing around cereal box templates and cutting with scissors. Did rotary cutters even exist then?

All of my quilts have been made by trial and error, the mistakes discovered along the way. But as mistakes were made, I have figured out easier ways to do things. Take-away appliqué grew out of that struggle to correct past mistakes. The unique way that I make biases developed from the struggle of doing it. Quilting without a frame or a hoop is the only way I have ever quilted, and I didn't have someone tell me that this was not the "correct" way. Now I know that there is less stress on my joints by lifting the quilt to my needle from underneath rather than rocking the needle through the quilt as you do using a frame or a hoop.

My advice to new quilters is *just get started*. Of course, now that I'm teaching around the country I love for people to sign up for classes, but don't WAIT for one—start making a quilt. Then the class will probably mean more and will help solve some of the problems that show up during the process of making your quilt.

I entered my first competitions to get judge's comments so that I could learn what I was doing right and what I was doing wrong. My first book, *Take-away Appliqué*, shows pictures of my appliquéd quilts until 1998 along with the critiques from the judges.

The judge's comments that helped me most were:

→ Pencil marks must be removed
→ Shadowing (*meaning that I appliquéd a light color fabric over a dark color and the dark fabric showed through the light fabric*)
→ Piecing could be more precise
→ More quilting in the appliqué is needed to add relief
→ Design elements could be better related
→ Two knots found on back
→ Miters off
→ Quilting stitches should be consistent in size
→ More color value change would be appreciated
→ Border treatment less imaginative than the rest
→ Consider scale of borders

Judges critiques have also been included in this book. Luckily, the newer quilts have fewer negative comments since I have tried to learn along the way. Reading the positive comments should help all of us know what kinds of things the judges look for when quilts are in competitions.

This book is titled *Adventure & Appliqué* because a lot of the sewing on my quilts was done while traveling. Also, many of the designs in the quilts were inspired by things that Garland and I saw on our trips. Looking for quilt designs and ideas has become second nature to me. The Art Nouveau building facades in Prague are an inspiration to me as well as the sewer covers on the sidewalks in Japan! And searching a library in a different country is often rewarding as well.

Sewing tips have been included, many becoming obvious to me as I made mistakes along the way.

Baste some appliqué on a block, fold it up along with thread, needle, scissors, and thimble, and off you go ... adventure & appliqué, what could be better than that?

Paths Taken...
Lessons Learned Along the Way

As a scientist, my husband, Garland, often travels the world giving lectures and consulting with former students. Our children are now grown, which often leaves me the opportunity to accompany him, especially when he's globe trekking to an exotic and intriguing destination.

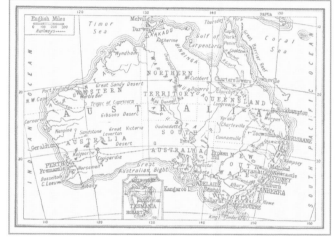

In 1998 we visited Brisbane, Australia—a beautiful city along the curved banks of the Brisbane River. While Garland worked at the university, I explored the city by river ferries.

I have found that seeing the sights and smelling the smells of a new place often feed my imagination. Not surprising, my main objective while in Brisbane was to look for a new idea for a quilt. I found a real treasure in a Brisbane library, a rare addition of Alexander Pushkin's *Tale of Tsar Saltan, of his Son, the Famous and Mighty Hero Prince Guidon Saltanovich, and of the Beautiful Swan Princess* with illustrations by the famous Russian folktale illustrator Ivan Bilibin (ca.1905).

The story of Tsar Saltan is one of transformation and earthy creatures. Through his odyssey, our hero, Prince Guidon, morphs into a mosquito, a fly, and a bee, all before falling in love with a princess who has herself morphed from a swan. In LONG AGO AND FAR AWAY we see the "beautiful Swan Princess" lying in the grass amongst the living creatures. I spent hours playing with my collection of appliqué designs, transforming the grass into a menagerie of flowers, birds, reptiles, and of course my favorite thing to appliqué, insects.

Long Ago and Far Away ✦ 54" × 72" ✦ 1998

The colors of Long Ago and Far Away are vivid. They have to be in order to match the whimsy, magic, and intrigue of the Russian fairy tale, which indirectly inspired this quilt. Long Ago and Far Away received the first prize in innovative appliqué at the International Quilt Festival in Houston as well as awards from the Mid-Atlantic Quilt Festival, Williamsburg, Virginia; the Quilter's Heritage Celebration, Lancaster, Pennsylvania; Rockome Gardens, Arcola, Illinois; and University City, Missouri.

The judges speak their minds ...

- Imagery at lower part slightly less clear
  (Does that mean that all of my efforts to include my favorite living things in the grass didn't quite work out?)
- Love the flowers and critters
- I love the details in this quilt
- Represents every tale told
- I want to go into this picture— color and design are total perfection
- I could look at it for hours
- Tremendous details
- Black embroidery enhances
- Wide integration of skills
- Love the flowers and critters
- Wonderful energetic design
- Coat is dynamite

The quilt was made in thirds beginning with the princess in the grass. I then made the city, followed by the prince, and lastly the appliqué joining the top and bottom of the quilt.

LONG AGO AND FAR AWAY • 54" x 72" • 1998

Suzanne Marshall → Adventure & Appliqué

SEWING TIP

I was using a damp cloth to wash out the water-soluble pen marks when the dye of one of the red flags ran down the blue sky. Oh no! What to do? My friend and fellow quilter Carolyn Birge suggested that I use a bit of Synthrapol® soap when washing the quilt to see if the red that bled would come out. It did! Hooray!

Now when I start to make a quilt that contains colors that MIGHT run, I cut two-inch patches of each suspicious fabric, place them across a piece of muslin, and quickly machine sew a line down the middle. I then dip the fabric with the patches in water and let it drip-dry over the bathtub. Whenever I find a fabric that bleeds and leaves a trace of dye along the muslin, I eliminate that fabric from the quilt.

I decided on a border that fit the Art Nouveau time period of my original illustration. The flowing corners frame the quilt nicely, perfectly fitting the ornate yet earthy scene.

OPPOSITE LEFT: *The border appliqué needed embroidery to show the ins and outs of the design.*

Garland shares his thoughts ...

Suzanne has been concerned about using images from the past in her quilts. My advice has been that she should always acknowledge the sources of her inspiration, always make the image her own by adding or deleting, and modify the colors, patterns, borders, and placement to render the resulting image as novel. Besides, she generally works in a different media (quilts) than the original (mosaics, tapestries, embroideries, rugs, etc.). Finally, she should not exploit the image commercially without checking with the source.

Artists have used previous designs as inspiration for centuries. Should there have only been one Madonna and Child? Cass Gilbert, the architect for the St. Louis Art Museum and designer of the lampposts that inspired Suzanne's quilt CASS GILBERT REMEMBERED, used similar bas-relief motifs we once saw carved in marble at the Etruscan Museum in Rome. Artists receive inspiration from the visual images they see; what's fun is how they change or juxtapose those images in novel ways. ❧

ADORATION OF THE MAGI ✦ 55" x 63" ✦ 1999

ADORATION OF THE MAGI was inspired by a seventeenth-century Norwegian devotional tapestry. The design came together perfectly in my mind's eye when I crossed paths with the consummate orange fabric. This quilt has won prizes in Houston, at the International Quilt Festival, as well as in University City, Missouri.

The judges speak their minds ...

- Balance of design needs improvement
- Bound edge wobbles a bit
- Conveys a very European feel
- Very interesting symbols and mythological creatures
- Successful portrayal of theme
- All elements work together
- Intricate design well executed
- Appropriate fabric selections
- Lovely hand quilting

I love keeping ancient designs alive by adapting them to quilts. During the slow process of hand appliqué, I take time to find out all I can about the original pieces, all the while wondering about their makers from long ago.

Seventeenth-century Norwegian tapestries particularly intrigue me, but it was the cover of the January 1998 issue of *HALI* magazine that truly caught my attention. There on the glossy page in front of me was a breathtaking tapestry, a linen and wool weaving dating from 1717 in the Gudbrandsdal Valley of Norway. The tapestry depicts the Adoration of the Magi, the three kings on horseback bringing gifts to the Christ child.

Wouldn't you know, I was wandering through my local quilt store when I came across an orange fabric that set off a buzzer in my head. It instantly reminded me of the picture from *HALI*. I knew that moment I had to transform the picture I had seen into fabric.

ADORATION OF THE MAGI • 55" x 63" • 1999

Suzanne Marshall → Adventure & Appliqué

This tapestry makes me smile. The background is dominated by a distorted octagon set off by strange folk-art creatures. In fact, the entire tapestry appears distorted and contains symbols that are still a mystery to me. My challenge was to make a quilt that would hang straight, and be straight, but look crooked!

Garland shares his thoughts ...

HALI, *the International Magazine for Fine Carpets and Textiles, is a bimonthly visual feast for the Marshalls. Suzanne usually finds quilt candidates in several issues each year and marks them so she can find them again. You will see quilts inspired by pictures from* HALI *throughout this book.*

During a trip to Norway in 2004, we were lucky enough to make an appointment with one of the curators in the Lillehammer Kunstmuseum. She brought out several antique tapestries, gave us white gloves to wear, and allowed us to help her unroll them for a close view. We were allowed to see the backs, gaze at the stitching up close, and to photograph them with flash, which was a surprise to me considering how faded some of them were.

ABOVE: *In the Lillehammer Art Museum – Norway*

Garland shares his thoughts …

This was our first trip to Norway, inspired by the desire to see original biblical wedding tapestries, and did we ever. The people at the museums in both Lillehammer and Oslo were both hospitable and appreciative of how Suzanne had done her homework on many of the tapestries and their histories.

Fifty-eight Norwegian tapestries depicting the Adoration of the Magi theme are known to exist. The tapestry that inspired my quilt is in the collection of the Museum of Applied Art in Oslo, Norway. Helen Kelley, a well-known quilter from Minnesota, also made a quilt adapted from another of the Adoration of the Magi tapestries. Her quilt was selected as one of the top 100 quilts of the twentieth century and contains livelier horses.

The Magi tapestry owned by the Kunstmuseum in Lillehammer is quite similar to the Magi tapestry in the Oslo museum, but the date on it is 1735. Since the weavers of the day used old tapestries as patterns, the 1717 tapestry may have been the model for the 1735 tapestry, because many of the other Magi tapestries are quite different. However, the fact that tapestries were more or less copied from other tapestries makes the woven dates unreliable, according to the curator of the Kunstmuseum.

SEWING TIP

The crooked stars were made by piecing the diamonds on the machine without sewing all of the way to the edge of the pieces. This left a seam allowance that could more easily be turned under when appliquéing to the background. ⚜

Adventure & Appliqué ← Suzanne Marshall

WHAT'S FOR DINNER? • 40" x 40" • 1999

Adventure & Appliqué ← Suzanne Marshall

WHAT'S FOR DINNER? ✦ 40" x 40" ✦ 1999

David Small from Artistic Fabrics invited me to design a small quilt for an invitational exhibit featuring his special hand-painted fabrics. I sent him a drawing of frogs on leaves. Not long after that I received an assortment of beautiful, hand-painted fabrics to be used specially for this quilt.

Adding a bug and a snail on the quilt might make the viewer think these critters were the frogs' dinner, but that is not where the name comes from. While making the quilt, time disappeared. Each day I became so absorbed in my sewing I didn't know what time it was. Before I knew it, Garland would show up in my sewing room saying, "What's for dinner?"

SEWING TIP

Hand-painted fabric is difficult to hand quilt, especially if small stitches are desired. ✿

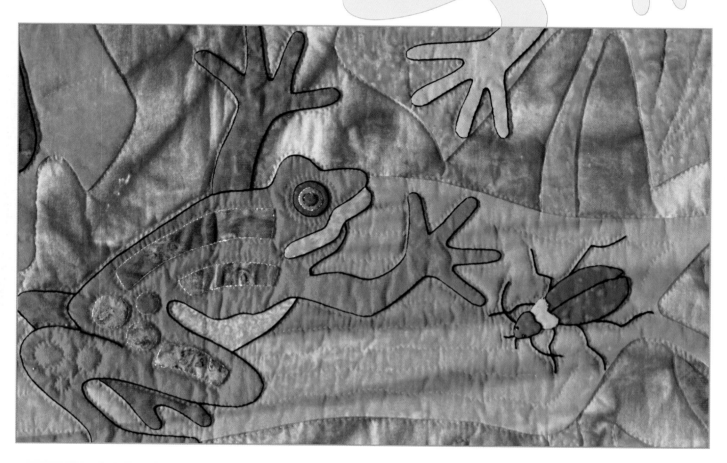

Bed Bugs ✦ *92" × 92"* ✦ *1992*

Adventure & Appliqué ✦ Suzanne Marshall

DON'T BUG ME ✦ 82" × 82" ✦ 1996

BED BUGS (1992) and DON'T BUG ME (1996) were such fun to make I decided to try my luck at a third bug quilt.

LEAF HOPPERS • 89" x 89" • 2000

Adventure & Appliqué ⪻ Suzanne Marshall

LEAF HOPPERS ✦ 89" x 89" ✦ 2000

LEAF HOPPERS has won several awards including Best of Show in the juried show in University City, Missouri.

The judges speak their minds …

- 🐝 Red lattice strips are not straight
- 🐝 Binding needs to be filled (*I thought I did, but maybe there was somewhere that was missing some batting.*)
- 🐝 Sashing too narrow for the size of the blocks
- 👑 Love the color scheme; orange really adds life to each of the blocks
- 👑 Delightful, wonderful blocks
- 👑 A surprise in every block
- 👑 Excellent workmanship and fine quilting
- 👑 Complementary border

The idea for LEAF HOPPERS was to use leaf shapes from a guidebook on tree identification and then to place bugs on the leaves. Many of the bug designs were adapted from a guidebook on the beetles of New Guinea.

A symmetrical design like the blocks in LEAF HOPPERS is easier than it looks. Only one-fourth of a block needs to be designed. It is then copied three more times to make the whole. See how easy it is for yourself. The templates and instructions for the "leaf hoppers" can be found on pages 110–127.

Garland shares his thoughts …

Suzanne was thrilled when her quilts (LEAF HOPPERS, AKIRA KONI-SHI, and DRAGONFLOWERS) were invited to be in the Thirty Distinguished Quilt Artists of the World exhibit curated by Robert Shaw and held in the Tokyo Dome Stadium in 2003. As we were unable to attend, we asked our dear friend Akemi Konishi (some readers will remember that Akemi was the source of all the Japanese yukata, summer kimono, fabrics from which Suzanne made several quilts including one of her three in Tokyo) if she could attend and take pictures for Suzanne. Akemi took the train to Tokyo from her home near Nagoya, and was one of over 250,000 attendees during the weeklong exhibit. To paraphrase Akemi, "I found a huge crowd of visitors in front of the AKIRA KONISHI quilt (coincidentally this quilt is named after her husband). I asked them what interested them the most, or how they felt about it. They said the AKIRA KONISHI quilt was very American, and yet very Japanese because of the yukata patterns in blue and white, and because of the tranquility it presented. The middle-aged or elder visitors said they missed the traditional yukata fabrics which had been disappearing in the kimono market."

RIGHT: *Our friend Akemi Konishi photographed my quilts at the Thirty Distinguished Quilt Artists of the World exhibit in Tokyo, Japan (2003).*

QUILTS: *AKIRA KONISHI, DRAGONFLOWERS, and LEAF HOPPERS*

Adventure & Appliqué ❧ Suzanne Marshall

SEWING TIP

The black embroidery thread used for the bug legs did not show up well against leaves. To compensate, I added another row of outline stitch embroidery using metallic thread, which gave the bugs an eye-catching glitter and zest. Sometimes twice as much work is worth it! ⚜

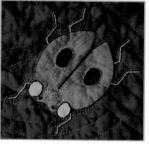

Peace • 43" x 65" • 2000

Adventure & Appliqué ← Suzanne Marshall

PEACE ✦ 43" × 65" ✦ 2000

Garland and I both love Art Nouveau designs. PEACE is one of Garland's absolute favorites.

The judges speak their minds …

- Next time consider a lighter green background behind human figure so the scales of green vary between inner quilt and border area
- Some surface distortion
- Off-centered design is effective
- Good fabric choices (*Apparently this judge didn't agree with the first negative comment made by another judge.*)
- Excellent hand quilting
- Lovely fabrics and color play
- Beautiful stitching

The first Art Nouveau quilt that I made for Garland, TOUJOURS NOUVEAU, won the Gingher Award for hand workmanship at the American Quilter's Society Quilt Show & Contest in Paducah, Kentucky, in 1993 and is in the collection of the Museum of the American Quilter's Society. Since we no longer own the quilt, I am always on the lookout for other Art Nouveau ideas.

A Dover book called *Treasury of Art Nouveau Design and Ornament,* selected by Carol Belanger Grafton, contains copyright-free line drawings, some of which are suitable for transformation to fabric. The design for PEACE is attributed to Ida F. Ravaison and was certainly designed at the turn of the twentieth century.

Though many people enjoy it, PEACE has never won an award. This is a testament to just how subjective quilting (like any art) can be. Just to look at the judges' comments, you can see that where one judge sees "lovely fabrics and color play," another judge sees a flaw. This is why it is so important that you make quilts to suit yourself and that speak to YOU.

PEACE

Garland shares his thoughts ...
Can you imagine the shocked look on Suzanne's face when she was notified that TOUJOURS NOUVEAU *was selected as one of the Twentieth Century's 100 Best American Quilts and later appeared at a special exhibit in Houston? Not bad for someone that never had a lesson!*

SEWING TIP

After I finished the last stitch of appliqué, I stepped back to appreciate my work, only to realize I didn't have a single bug or critter on the quilt. If you take a close look at the quilt, you may notice that oversight has been corrected. In the grass near the lady you will find quilted dragonflies, lizards, and snails.

Be sure to add a personal touch. If your unique element isn't found in the appliqué, add it in the quilting. In other words, make each quilt your own.

Garland shares his thoughts ...
As much as you try hard not to love one child more than another, this quilt is still one of my special favorites. It should be obvious from reading the judges' comments on Suzanne's quilts in this book that every quilt has its set of judges. PEACE *is still searching. The exceptional quality of the quilts entered in major shows these days makes the top choices of the judges subjective in nature. Every show I attend, I find some awards I don't understand, most I enthusiastically support, and a few quilts that just aren't my cup of tea. Guess that's why they haven't asked me to judge.* ⚜

TOUJOURS NOUVEAU ✦ 68" x 80" ✦ 1993

The first Art Nouveau quilt that I made for Garland, TOUJOURS NOUVEAU, won the Gingher Award for hand workmanship at the American Quilter's Society Quilt Show & Contest in Paducah, Kentucky, in 1993 and is in the collection of the Museum of the American Quilter's Society.

MOTHER'S DAY ✦ 81" X 81" ✦ 2001

What do you know? MOTHER'S DAY won the Timeless Treasures Award for best hand workmanship at the AQS Quilt Show & Contest in Paducah in 2002. What a fabulous surprise! So MOTHER'S DAY joined TOUJOURS NOUVEAU in the museum. What a thrill to see them hanging near each other when we visited the next year!

The judges speak their minds …

- ♕ Great attention to detail
- ♕ Mother's Day images very moving
- ♕ Appliqué, embroidery, quilting all first-rate
- ♕ Border complements design—nice balance
- ♕ Nicely done, indeed!

When traveling, I always like to have appliqué or quilting to take with me to work on. However, it can be challenging to design a project that is both interesting and portable.

The idea for MOTHER'S DAY came while I was searching through books of decorative patterns and building ornaments. My concept was that each quilt block would be formed by using only a portion of a decorative motif. Just as in the quilt LEAF HOPPERS, only a fourth of a block needed to be designed. By adding three additional copies, the block was completed.

The complex green border designs for the appliqué in each block were basted down. I needed only one spool of thread, scissors, needle, and a thimble to take my studio with me.

All of the green appliquéd borders in each block were finished on trips. Then the real challenge began! What would fit inside the complex borders, I asked myself, especially since the borders left different amounts of space in the middle of each block? Should I use hummingbirds? Butterflies? It was actually Garland who came up with the idea of adapting some Swiss Scherenschnitte designs.

The red color of the Scherenschnitte designs makes them stand out from the borders. The extra line of embroidery around the appliqués makes them really pop. With red in the middle of the quilt, the outside border also needed red to tie the design together.

All of the appliqué for MOTHER'S DAY was done on trips. When returning home, the appliqué was put away for the next trip. Because the quilt wasn't worked on continuously, and the hand quilting took about seven months (this was done at home due to the quilt's large size), the quilt took three years to make.

Garland shares his thoughts ...

I am lucky to have the vicarious joy, the pleasure of watching Suzanne struggle with a project. Her search for the inspiration of the next quilt is constant wherever she might be. She will spend hours selecting the right fabric from her stash, wondering if these colors really complement each other, redrawing a flower, or adding a beetle, trying out complex borders versus simple ones. And then, it comes together. Somehow Suzanne knows when to quit struggling and let the quilt be born. I witness the entire creative process unrolling before me.

SEWING TIP

Traveling is a great time to get some serious appliqué done. After all, what else would you rather be doing while stuck in a cramped airline seat?

Cut only the outside of the appliqué including seam allowance, then baste down. The ins and outs within the complicated appliqué can be cut just ahead of needle-turning to help eliminate fraying fabric, especially when being packed and unpacked during travel. ⚜

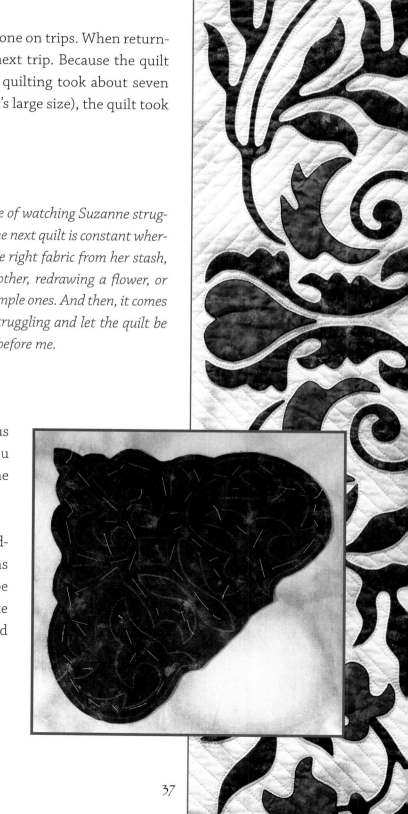

A MIDSUMMER'S DREAM ✦ 17" × 72" ✦ 2001

Amazing! I was approached by Opal Frey from the Rocky Mountain Quilt Museum in Golden, Colorado, to have a retrospective exhibit in one of their galleries. Opal sent me a drawing of the gallery space. Lo and behold, there was a tall, skinny wall that jutted out from the rest of the space. None of my quilts would fit that space, so I decided to make one that would! The quilt did fit the space perfectly in the museum, which made me happy.

A MIDSUMMER'S DREAM won second prize in the small art quilt category at the 2001 International Quilt Festival in Houston, Texas.

The judges speak their minds …

- Avoid dark fabric showing through light fabric on binding (*shadowing—that sounds familiar*)
- Wonderful design
- Excellent overall quilt

The inspiration for A MIDSUMMER'S DREAM sprouted from a line drawing in *Borders, Frames, and Decorations of the Art Nouveau Period*, a Dover book of copyright-free illustrations. This quilt, however, would not be half as interesting without the luxurious piece of hand-dyed fabric by Artfabrik. At that time the company was owned by Melody Johnson and Laura Wasilowski, and is now owned exclusively by Laura (www.artfabrik.com).

I changed the drawing in several ways in order to fit my tastes. For one, the original outside border had protruding flowers from the edge, which I didn't like, so I redrew the flowers as well as the Art Nouveau squiggles between the leaves. The big dragonfly is accompanied by small dragonflies in my quilt. The flowers between the snail and the frog have been transformed. And I HAD to add a bug!

Adventure & Appliqué ✦ Suzanne Marshall

In 2001, I entered this quilt at the International Quilt Festival in Houston under the small art quilt category. There were 72 quilts in that category. I think mine may have been the only hand-quilted piece. First prize was won by Melody Johnson using her (Artfabrik's) hand-dyed fabric. Second prize was won by A Midsummer's Dream, using Artfabrik's wonderfully dyed fabric; and third prize was won by Melody Johnson using her hand-dyed fabric. We don't have to guess what the judges liked! Because of its strange size, that's the only competition I've entered with A Midsummer's Dream.

A Midsummer's Dream

It's amazing how easy it was to work on a narrow quilt, something I'd never experienced before! This quilt accompanied me on plane trips. Since I don't use a frame or a hoop when hand quilting, it was very easy to do while traveling.

One plane trip was not only memorable, but delicious as well. Garland and I flew to San Francisco while I was in the process of hand quilting A Midsummer's Dream. The head flight attendant in first class happened to be interested in quilts. She kept coming back to talk, and as often happens, we knew some quilters in common. Eventually she brought back a plastic bag with a bottle of white wine in it. Picture this. We were sitting in the third from last row next to the lavatories in economy class, scrunched in with the other uncomfortable folks on a rather full flight. Then she brought another plastic bag filled with eight small bottles of liqueurs—two bottles each of Bailey's® Irish Cream, Kahlúa®, amaretto, and brandy, as well as packages of smoked almonds. For the pièce de résistance, she brought us cups of chocolate-covered balls filled with cherry ice cream. We sat there licking our lips and spoons. One woman near the rear of the plane exclaimed, "I've never seen that before!" Nothing like a quilt to break the ice.

SEWING TIP

When your background fabric has a graduated color, reverse the direction of the fabric while you are making an inner strip. Separate the main part of the quilt from the outside border with color gradation going the opposite way. ⚜

This is the Chinese mandarin badge Garland bought in Hong Kong with his Cathay Award prize money. Gorgeous... isn't it.

FIRST RANK ✦ 46" x 46" ✦ 2001

This quilt utilizes quintessential Mandarin Chinese iconography to embrace the medium of appliqué. FIRST RANK has received some special awards, including first place in wall quilts at both Quilter's Heritage Celebration, in Lancaster, Pennsylvania, and Sew Near to My Heart in Cincinnati, Ohio.

The judges speak their minds ...

- A couple of corners on binding need improvement
- Vary quilting motifs
- Wonderful presentation of a complex design
- Excellent supportive quilting
- Colors and fabrics well-chosen for quilt style
- Very well-balanced design
- Appropriate use of embroidery
- Border appropriate to piece
- Workmanship excellent

In the summer of 2000, Garland and I went to China to attend the Chinese Peptide Symposium in Huangshan, in the Yellow Mountains. Garland was honored to receive the Cathay Award—the first non-Chinese to be selected.

While in China we became acquainted with Chinese mandarin badges. These are beautifully embroidered pieces of silk with meticulous stitches, many needing a magnifying glass to see the individual stitches. The mandarins wore them on their robes to indicate either civil or military rank.

For thirteen centuries, difficult examinations were given to male recruits for service to the emperor of China. For those who passed, there were nine possible ranks in either the military or in administration. Civil ranks were identified by different birds—a different variety for each rank. Military squares used real or mythological animals to designate rank. The top civil rank was the crane—a Chinese symbol of longevity and wisdom associated with advanced age.

Many mandarin badges contained the sun disk, which may have represented the emperor, the Son of Heaven. Or another thought is that the sun represents the Chinese proverb "Aim at the sun and rise high."

Ladder to the Clouds; Intrigue and Tradition in Chinese Rank, by Beverley Jackson and David Hugus PhD, is a comprehensive and informative book on Chinese mandarins and their badges of rank. Garland used his prize money from the Cathay Award to purchase a lovely old Chinese mandarin badge in Hong Kong, as a wonderful reminder of our trip.

Garland shares his thoughts ...

Once again, a visual image struck a cord in Suzanne and led to a whole education about Chinese culture. It's hard to predict what image will resonate within Suzanne and set her off in a new direction.

Some of the judges comments regarding the quilting of FIRST RANK have made me think about the state of contemporary quilting. I'm starting to wonder if the popularity of machine quilting, which in stiff competitions is very closely and finely done, is now influencing the judging when looking at hand quilting. Regardless, our industry is certainly changing.

SEWING TIPS

Experiment with different threads. Wanting more emphasis on the crane's feathers than the DMC® embroidery floss that I usually use, I bought a German rayon needlepoint ribbon called Neon Rays. It was just the right amount of variation needed for the feathers. I'm still surprised that I could embroider with a rayon ribbon so effectively! ❧

Adventure & Appliqué ❧ Suzanne Marshall

THE ORCHARD ◆ 46" x 36½" ◆ 2002

THE ORCHARD features a cable design in the black border motif, historically popular in mosaics dating as early as the fourth century, from a Roman villa at Piazza Armenia in Sicily.

The judges speak their minds ...

- 🐾 I'm not sure about the contemporary design in the black border
- 🐾 Composition might be less intense—concentrated to give the viewer a resting place
- 👑 Very nice work on embroidery outline
- 👑 Love the whimsical nature of the quilt
- 👑 Beautiful; love the embroidery and details

Thumbing through a book containing British embroideries, *The Victoria and Albert Museum's Textile Collection: Embroidery in Britain from 1200 to 1750*, I found a photograph of a long cushion cover (ca 1600). The old embroidery is 20" x 41" in size and contains pear, cherry, and apple trees as well as huntsmen, gardeners, and insects. It sang "quilt" to me.

Two trees seemed like enough, so I cut off a tree and tried to adapt the rest of the embroidery to a quilt.

THE ORCHARD • 46" x 36½" • 2002

THE ORCHARD

THE ORCHARD has not won a prize, but has been shown in a local juried competition. Perhaps that is in part because this quilt is designed with an eye towards historical accuracy rather than the aesthetic standards of modern design.

Garland shares his thoughts …

Suzanne has a love for folk art, regardless of culture. She finds an image in a book or magazine, from a church mosaic or tapestry, modifies it for fabric, and makes the quilt her own through her choices of fabrics, embellishments (embroidery, for example), deletions and additions to the image, etc. If one is going to spend any time at all making a quilt, it seems to me that adapting it to your own vision is essential. It then becomes a major creative outlet for the quiltmaker, rather than just mere handwork.

SEWING TIP

Each multi-pieced appliqué motif was a cinch to do using the take-away appliqué technique for pattern placement. You can find a more detailed explanation of the technique on pages 101–104. ❧

Adventure & Appliqué ❦ Suzanne Marshall

The Wise and Foolish Virgins • 47" x 57" • 2002

Adventure & Appliqué ← Suzanne Marshall

THE WISE AND FOOLISH VIRGINS ✦ 47" x 57" ✦ 2002

The wise and foolish virgins were historically a popular tapestry theme, particularly for wedding gifts or as a portion of a woman's dowry. My design has won first prize in wall quilts at Quilter's Heritage Celebration in Lancaster, Pennsylvania, as well as second prize at the International Quilt Festival in Houston.

The judges speak their minds …

- 🐕 Slight dog-ears on corners
- 👑 A design in a crowded space is difficult to do, but you have achieved this very successfully
- 👑 Great value contrast
- 👑 Yellow inner border provides good separation
- 👑 Workmanship excellent
- 👑 Fabric colors and patterns are perfect
- 👑 Fabulous quilt

The most popular theme for seventeenth-century Norwegian tapestries was the New Testament parable of the wise and foolish virgins. Seventy-three of these tapestries are known to exist. Many are thought to have been wedding gifts or were part of a woman's dowry. They show the virgins depicted as brides wearing seventeenth-century dress and Norwegian bridal crowns. Used as bedspreads,

the tapestries were wonderful mementos of the bridal couple's own wedding and also served to illustrate parables and moral principles for the family. The 82" x 61" bedspread tapestry that inspired my quilt, THE WISE AND FOOLISH VIRGINS, is owned by the Minneapolis Institute of Arts. (For more information about the Minneapolis tapestry, see *Euro-*

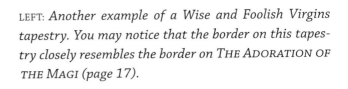

LEFT: *Another example of a Wise and Foolish Virgins tapestry. You may notice that the border on this tapestry closely resembles the border on THE ADORATION OF THE MAGI (page 17).*

pean Tapestry in the Minneapolis Institute of Arts by Candace J. Adelson, distributed by Harry N. Abrams Inc., Publishers.)

Roughly translated, the inscription on the particular tapestry that served as inspiration for my quilt says "when five virgins were wise, five were foolish year AM 63." Curiously, in many of the Norwegian tapestries, inscriptions between the horizontal rows of virgins are upside down or backwards. It is thought the reversals may have occurred because many of the weavers were illiterate and perhaps used other tapestries for patterns, placing them behind the warp or reversing existing tapestries to use as models for new pieces. The fact that there exists a completely reversed copy of the Minneapolis tapestry from which I designed my quilt lends credibility to that theory.

When we visited the Lillehammer Kunstmuseum in Norway, we learned from the curator that as time went by, the tapestries started losing some of their religious significance. The wise and foolish virgins apparently always used to have the "bridegroom" (Christ) in the panel with the wise virgins and the oil seller in the panel with the foolish virgins. My quilt doesn't have the oil seller, but you can still see which virgins are foolish because of the way the lamps are held. We saw one tapestry at the museum without either the bridegroom or oil seller, and one had the "virgins" all holding their lamps the same way. Fascinating!

There's another mystery I pondered while appliquéing the borders on my quilt using my take-away appliqué technique. One border was very different from the other three! The left border has a background for the appliqué, while the other three do not. Three of the borders contain either birds or an animal; the left does not, but does contain several little four-patch designs. Fortunately, the St. Louis Art Museum contains a wonderful library that allowed me to research this mystery. It is thought that perhaps a tapestry called THE WISDOM OF SOLOMON was started on the loom, but after only the left border was completed, the weaving was interrupted and continued on as THE WISE AND FOOLISH VIRGINS. ❧

Two portions of THE WISE AND FOOLISH VIRGINS border.

Autumn Fest ✦ 21½" × 69" ✦ 2003

No, it's not Jack and the Beanstalk! This long, skinny quilt depicts apple picking from long ago. The design is adapted from several woodblocks found in various editions of *The Book of Hours* (ca 1500). I like making narrow quilts, as they are so easy to quilt on trips!

The judges speak their minds …

- Pencil marks in outer border should be removed
- Very nice embroidery stitching to help bring out figures
- Nice craftsmanship

SEWING TIP

When sewing apples or other circles, turn under only enough seam allowance to make one stitch at a time. ⚜

Arabesque • 63" x 84" • 2004

Adventure & Appliqué ⚑ Suzanne Marshall

ARABESQUE ✦ *63" x 84"* ✦ 2004

Arabesque is designed to have the vivid and luxurious character of a Persian carpet but with the feel of a quilt. It has won a couple of honorable mentions and judge's choice in national competitions. It won a first prize at a juried show in University City, Missouri.

The judges speak their minds …

- Design elements seem just a little crowded on the background
- Could have left more space for the eye to rest
- Bold colors work well with design; beautiful quilting stitch
- Looks like an oriental carpet *(wonder why?)*
- Exciting color combinations
- Motif and colors are good representation of the design source
- Use of gold thread enhances appliqué
- Striking; embroidery details add a nice touch

HALI magazine continues to be a wonderful source of inspiration for me. Published in London, *HALI* is an international magazine of fine carpets and textiles. The name derives from the Turkish word for carpet, which has survived unchanged for over a thousand years. A yearly subscription can be expensive; however, issues can be found in museum libraries and carpet stores.

In a 1991 issue of *HALI*, a particularly wonderful carpet was advertised for auction to be held at the esteemed Sotheby's auction house. The carpet (ca 1905) was designed by John Henry Dearle and measured 14 ft. 10 in. by 11 ft. 6 in. The auction estimated the carpet between $100,000 to $150,000. I wonder how much it sold for? I wonder what it might be worth now?

I loved the carpet, and thought it could be adapted to a quilt. Changes were made, of course, including color. And I had to add birds and snails. As I drew out the design, the medallions changed as well as the border. At least the picture of the carpet got me started!

ARABESQUE was made in quarters, the medallions appliquéd after the quarters were joined. The medallions are large enough that they nearly obscure the seam lines.

John Henry Dearle (1860–1932) was inspired by motifs on classical Persian carpets and started working with William Morris in 1878. His carpet patterns are quite different in style from the Morris Arts and Crafts designs with larger repeats and a more Persian flavor.

SEWING TIP

Since some backgrounds are too large to easily hold while appliquéing, try dividing the background in portions—then join sections when most of the appliqué is finished.

I learned an expensive lesson when purchasing fabric for this quilt. I bought a gorgeous navy print for the background. I returned home and immediately started the quilt. After painstakingly cutting the pieces to the proper size and doing some careful and tedious markings, I began the appliqué. After completing several appliqué motifs, I realized that the weave was so dense I could hardly get my needle through it. It occurred to me how difficult hand quilting would be if I had that much difficulty with the appliqué. So I went back to the store and bought a different background. It was better to lose a week of work and the cost of five yards of fabric than to struggle through the entire making of the quilt. ❖

Adventure & Appliqué ❧ Suzanne Marshall

TOAD BOY ✦ 56½" × 23" ✦ 2004

Here we go again—another long skinny quilt, only this time the design runs vertically rather than horizontally. TOAD BOY was inspired by a picture in *The Studio*, a popular British magazine from the turn of the twentieth century. Because of its popularity at the time, many of the magazine's designs were Art Nouveau.

The judges speak their minds ...

- Edge of quilt should be straight
- Color impact could be improved
- Very realistic frogs
- Appliqué technique very good
- Good quilting stitch
- Binding well done
- Well balanced design
- Very original
- Colors and fabrics well chosen

If you take a look at the judges' comments, you might like to know that both the "colors and fabrics well chosen" and "color impact could be improved" comments were received in Houston at the same show. I always smile when I see that judges don't agree with each other! The lesson here is, always follow your own heart.

SEWING TIP

The boy has only four pieces: body, one arm (the one with the elbow sticking out), breechcloth, and hair. The rest of the detail is outline-stitch embroidery. Define detail with embroidery to enhance the quilt.

Sometimes it's easier to work with one strand of embroidery thread rather than two strands. The toads and boy have two strands outlining the appliqué. The leaves and stems have one strand. ❧

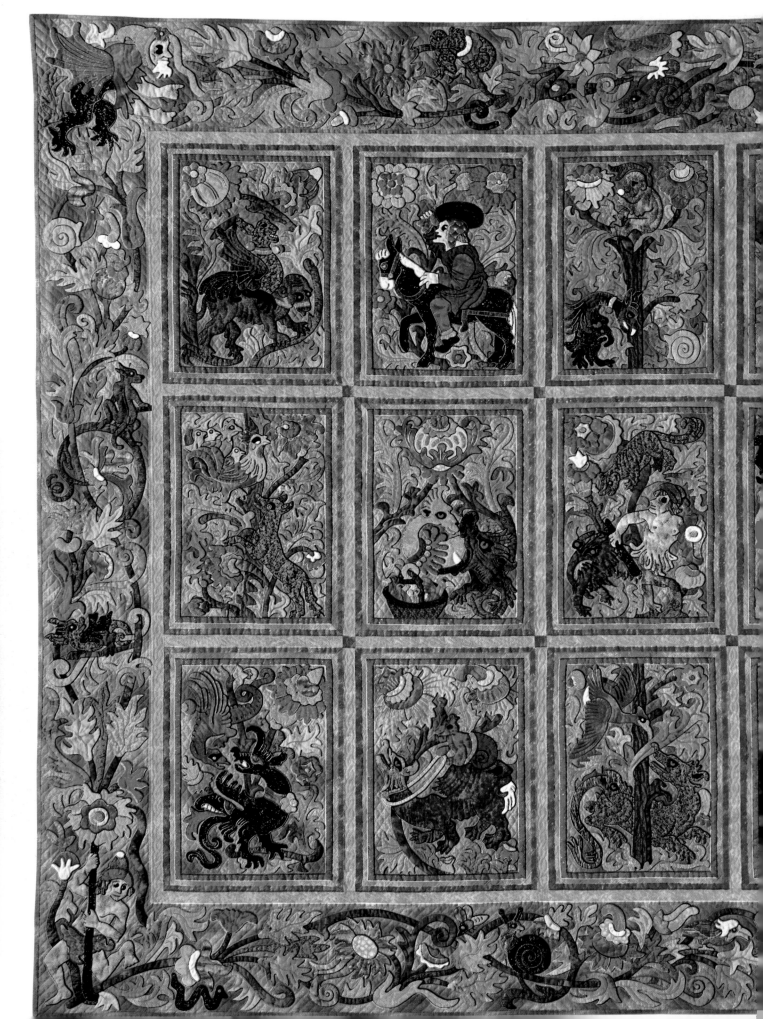

VISIONS ✦ 82" x 83" ✦ 2003

Garland shares his thoughts …

To keep the family entertained, Suzanne will often hold naming contests as she nears the completion of a quilt. "Visions" had its advocates (for example, Suzanne), but I loved the double-entendre of our son Lee's suggestion, "Out-of-Print." The images of this quilt are actually printers' ornaments from out-of-date books.

VISIONS has won prizes in Houston, Paducah, Minnesota (Best in Show), Pennsylvania, and New Hampshire.

The judges speak their minds …

- Binding needs to be fuller
- Remove quilting design marks
  (*I thought I did. Oh dear!*)
- In some places I'd like to see more value contrast, but embroidered outlining partly compensates for that
- If I only had three days to look at this quilt, I might see it all
- Design is stunning; beautiful quilt and appliqué technique
- Embroidery adds incredible depth; one to three rows of embroidery stitching around appliqué elements are very effective
- Composition of densely designed blocks handled well
- Ambitious design
- Wonderful bold color combinations; outstanding fabric selections

RIGHT: *Look what a difference embroidery makes.*

VISIONS was definitely a travel quilt; however, the appliqué was mostly done at home because of the complexity of the design. The added embroidery around each appliqué was my mindless airplane work. In some cases there are two rows of different colored embroidery threads around a piece.

The biggest challenge with VISIONS was designing the border. I wanted the borders to all be different but still so similar, that it might not be obvious until closely inspected.

Looking back on the process, I remember a rather bad experience. I had just a bit more embroidery to do on the blocks. I had figured out how to set them together, which enabled me to do the math and cut the outside border fabric in strips. We had a trip coming up, so I started the appliqué on the borders, leaving the setting of the blocks for a later time at home. I like doing as much appliqué on the border strips as possible before adding them to the quilt, then mitering the corners before adding the appliqué that covers the miters.

We got back from our trip, and I started putting patchwork triangles around the blocks. I finished four of them. They looked terrible! The triangles were so busy! They took away from the complicated designs in the blocks. I had to redesign the setting for the blocks, which ended up making the calculations for the amount of fabric needed for the borders completely wrong! Luckily, I had cut borders a bit longer than I actually needed, thus I had enough fabric but had to redraw all of the corners on each side. Groan!

Another story about VISIONS comes to mind. At Quilter's Heritage Celebration in Lancaster, Pennsylvania, it won a Best Workmanship award. As I went

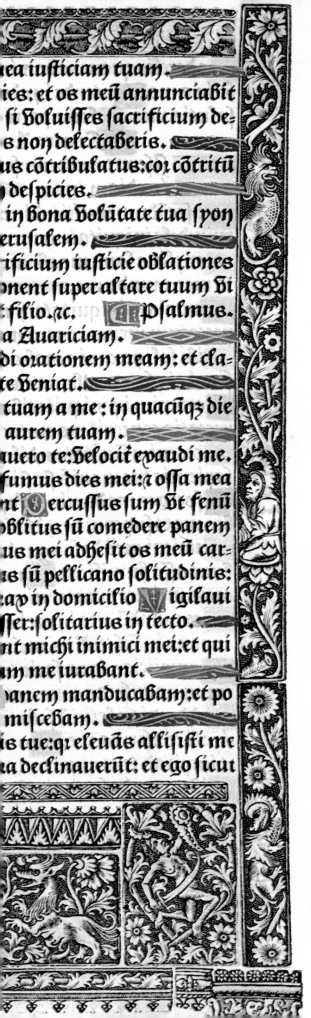

on the stage to stand by my quilt, my eyes were riveted by a *thread* coming out of the quilt right at my 5'2" vision level. I hoped no one would see me try to pick it off, *but it wouldn't come off of the quilt!* What was it? A loose quilting thread? How terrible to have a ribbon for workmanship on a quilt with a visible thread coming out of it. I thought to myself, *I have to try to find a way to get that thread off before it's shipped straight from the show in Lancaster to the AQS show in Paducah.* After teaching one afternoon I went to the exhibit with scissors in my pocket. I was really afraid the "quilt police" would come after me if they saw me head for a quilt with a pair of scissors! I loitered around the quilt until the crowds died down a bit. I found another teacher and asked her to shield me while I cut off the thread. Whew! My scissors quickly went back in my pocket.

Ancient printer's ornaments inspired Visions. I loved the two-headed beasts and gargoyle-type creatures. I laughed while I was appliquéing the strange beings. Is it two-headed? Is it a beard or a tail? I later discovered that the printer's ornaments were from woodblocks found in *The Book of Hours*, many editions of which were published in France around 1500. The woodblocks were printed next to the prayers as page decorations and were used multiple times within the same book.

CENTER: *A single leaf from* Book of Hours *(use of Rouen). Printed for Symon Vostre in Paris, 1508.*

𝒢arland shares his thoughts …

VISIONS (or as some would have it "OUT-OF PRINT") led us on an exciting adventure. Recently, Suzanne checked out a book on illuminated manuscripts that contained a page from a Book of Hours *printed in Paris by Philippe Pigouchet for Symon Vostre, a prominent publisher of* Book of Hours. *Several of the woodcut printer's ornaments she had used were on that single page.*

Research shows that the figures chosen by Suzanne for VISIONS *had been used in many of the different editions of* Book of Hours *printed by Pigouchet in Paris around 1500. Books printed within 50 years of the* Gutenberg Bible *(September 30, 1452) are referred to as "incunabula," a word I had seen, but never knew its exact meaning. As we were about to depart for a trip to Europe including a symposium at Oxford University, I checked their library catalog over the Web and learned they had at least eight* Book of Hours *printed by Pigouchet from 1498 to 1510. Two scientific colleagues at Oxford paved the way for Suzanne to become a "reader" at the Bodleian library with access to the rare book collection.*

While I attended my meeting, Suzanne surrounded herself with eight Book of Hours *printed by Pigouchet, studying the many different printer's ornaments by the same woodcut artist used to decorate pages. That must have been, without a doubt, the best scientific meeting she has ever attended with me.*

SEWING TIP

When cutting fabric for borders, cut more than needed in case adjustments need to be made. ✣

Adventure & Appliqué ✦ Suzanne Marshall

THE WANDERING HOUSEWIFE ✦ 47½" × 44½" ✦ 2005

THE WANDERING HOUSEWIFE is modeled after a picture of a Swiss tapestry. Once again, *HALI* enchanted me into making a quilt. THE WANDERING HOUSEWIFE won first prize in the pictorial wall quilt category in University City, Missouri.

The judges speak their minds ...

- ♛ Great images and arrangement
- ♛ Great combination of fabrics and colors and design
- ♛ The more you look, the more there is; this is wonderful—you have captured the personality of each character
- ♛ Black embroidery sets everything off nicely
- ♛ Great border; border enhances
- ♛ Fabulous workmanship
- ♛ Fun, humorous design and creatures

While flipping through the pages of *HALI*, I came across a picture of this Swiss tapestry. It sang quilt to me. To look at it, I couldn't help but laugh.

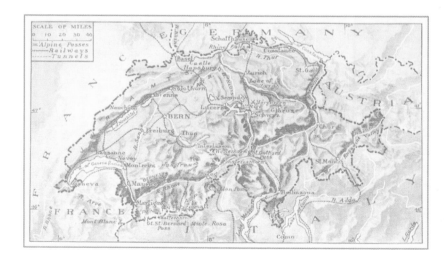

There were several Swiss satirical tapestries made around the same time which relate to a woman being "too busy" to bother with matters unrelated to the smooth running of her household. These tapestries were made to demonstrate the all-importance of marriage. This tapestry, only 27" x 35", was woven of wool and linen. Due to its size, it is thought to have been a cushion cover.

I entered THE WANDERING HOUSEWIFE in the Quintessential Quilt Exhibit sponsored by the Historical Society of University City, Missouri, and directed by the Circle in the Square Quilters (my local guild) with support of the St. Louis Regional Arts Commission. This exhibit, held every odd year, is the only judged and juried competition in the St. Louis area. For the month of the show, quilts are hung in the University City Public Library, which reaches many viewers who would not regularly attend quilt shows.

While the quilt was hanging in the exhibit, I received a call from a man who happened upon the exhibit and wanted to buy my quilt. I told him an astronomical price (since I didn't want to sell it), and he, thankfully, didn't buy it. I asked him why he wanted it. He said that he liked the colors. Hmm, I thought, and couldn't help but wonder if there was a "wandering housewife" in his life.

SEWING TIP

Letters in the alphabet can be patterned after different font styles on the computer. Just enlarge the selected font to the desired size. ⚜

THE GRIFFIN ✦ 52" x 32" ✦ 2005

Now I know why so many of my students love making smaller quilts. It really does take less time to finish them! THE GRIFFIN was adapted from a William de Morgan tile that is 8" x 16" in size.

The griffin in the quilt was appliquéd using the take-away appliqué method of pattern placement. It was easier to make small sections of the animal out of notebook paper rather than the whole beast at once. ✤

AND DRAGONS, TOO ... • 73½ x 92" • 2006

Adventure & Appliqué ← Suzanne Marshall

AND DRAGONS, TOO ... ✦ *73½" x 92"* ✦ *2006*

AND DRAGONS, TOO... is inspired by the work of master tile and ceramic designer William de Morgan (1839–1917), who was himself inspired largely by Middle Eastern art. AND DRAGONS, TOO... won two prizes at the IQA show in Houston and Indiana as well as first place at the AQS Quilt Show & Contest in Paducah, Kentucky.

The judges speak their mind ...

- A very "busy" appearance; difficult to settle your eye
- Needs more accurately aligned sashing
- Take care with triple-pieced border around squares; should be straight
- Nice embroidery details
- Good overall workmanship
- Quilting very nice, well chosen and well executed
- Excellent visual impact
- Outstanding use of color
- Colors and fabrics well chosen for quilt
- Creative use of pattern
- Bindings full and well applied
- Very good quilting
- Visual impact; color and fabric choices wonderful
- Use of color (warm colors juxtaposed with cool ones) is excellent; good use of bright (lime green, orange) as accents
- Embroidery stitches are even and lie smooth; embroidery adds another dimension
- Great balance of design in every block

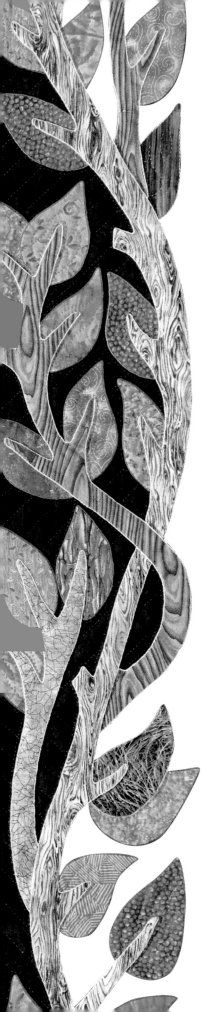

In June of 2004, I tagged along with Garland who had lectures to give in London. I spent my days in museums, always with an eye out for something I could use in my quilts. At the Victoria and Albert Museum, I found some old tiles by William de Morgan. At the time of his death, his wife bequeathed his drawings to the Victoria and Albert Museum, although it is thought that the collection is not complete. I had an immediate emotional response to those tiles. The quilt light bulb flashed on! AND DRAGONS, TOO... is an adaptation of some of de Morgan's tiles.

There were a few tiles with leaves on them, so I tried drawing branches with leaves on all of the designs that I used in the quilt. Most of the tiles were six-inch squares. The quilt blocks that I made are sixteen square inches, which left ample room for added detail.

Adventure & Appliqué ❦ Suzanne Marshall

Is it obvious that the borders on the sides of the quilt are wider than at the top and bottom? There was such a difference between the width and length of the quilt that I altered the border to keep proportion. I didn't want the quilt to be even longer by another two inches.

SEWING TIP

The branches are several different browns and prints, especially along the borders, as I had run out of my favorite fabrics by that time. By using many different prints in the same color range, different patterns and fabrics can be purchased to add to a quilt without it being obvious that you may not have enough of some of the fabrics. ❧

THE TANG TANGO ✦ *66½" x 71½"* ✦ *2006*

This design began with a Chinese valance, though you'd hardly recognize it now. THE TANG TANGO won a blue ribbon for overall craftsmanship at A Quilter's Gathering in Nashua, New Hampshire.

The judges speak their minds …

- ♛ Outline embroidery a good accent
- ♛ Well balanced
- ♛ Effective focal point
- ♛ Thread colors for quilting well chosen
- ♛ Good attention to detail
- ♛ Very good quilting stitch

THE TANG TANGO was inspired by a drawing from a portion of an eighth-century Chinese valance. I enlarged the drawing, then traced the enlargement. I didn't like portions of the center medallion, so I changed some of it. I also didn't like the corner designs, so I redesigned them. This led to the rest of the design changing as well.

Looking at my new design, I realized that I needed to incorporate some of the elements from the corners into the center medallion, so the center changed again! At least I left the Chinese goats in roundel form.

It is interesting to note that a parallel exists between the Chinese valance, a silk samite fabric from China, the Liao dynasty (ca 10th – 11th century), and a silver-gilt box from China dated 1024. How fascinating that an eighth-century design from the Tang dynasty continues to inspire other art throughout the centuries.

THE TANG TANGO

The quilt was appliquéd in quarters, adding the medallion and flower designs over the seams after joining the pieces. I must admit that I had lots of fun making the quilt until about the last quarter. By then I was bored with appliquéing the same design for a fourth time!

SEWING TIP

Many quilters think they need to match the color of the quilting thread with the fabric being quilted. I like using a different color of quilting thread so that I can more easily see the quilting and what is left to be quilted. ❧

Adventure & Appliqué ← Suzanne Marshall

SURPRISE • 40" x 55" • 2007

Adventure & Appliqué ↞ Suzanne Marshall

SURPRISE ✦ 40" x 55" ✦ 2007

SURPRISE was inspired by a drawing by William de Morgan, possibly used for a tile design. Seeing a snake amidst lilies and flowers is rather unusual. Hopefully the "surprise" in the design makes you chuckle.

The judges speak their minds …

♛ Exuberant design; embroidery adds to overall effect

In the spring of 2006, Garland and I took an adventure trip to New Guinea. By that time I had finished the appliqué on SURPRISE, so I took it along as my "travel quilt," which in hindsight was very poetic. I needed to embroider around all of the appliquéd motifs, which is perfect work for a long trip. Embroidery and quilting can be meditative and soothing.

Our first night in New Guinea, we had to spend the night in Mount Hagen in order to catch our plane to the Sepik River area—actually a lodge on the Karawari, a tributary of the Sepik. After dinner that night, Garland was in bed reading his book, and I decided to go back to the bar to take a picture of a mask that I liked. There were four men and a woman in the bar. The men started talking to me. Gibson, a worker at our hotel in Mt. Hagen, had five wives and wanted lots of sons to back him up in clan wars. He pulled up his shirtsleeve to show me his sliced bicep wound from a spear. Another man pulled up his pants legs to show me his wound. Another man pointed to a scar on his face. THAT was my introduction to clan warfare!!

The next morning we saw nothing of Mount Hagen because our guide said it was too dangerous to get outside of the barbed wire walls around the hotel. Later, eighteen of us filed into a small plane—even smaller than the small planes you may be imagining—and we took off over the densest jungle I've ever seen. The mountains were filled with jungle, not houses, not roads, not rivers, nothing but jungle. A short time into the flight, we started smelling fuel in the plane. The scent grew very strong, especially in the back where we were. In fact, our guide, Kevin, changed places with a woman in the back row who just couldn't breathe. I looked back at him and glanced at the trap door. It had liquid oozing into a puddle on the floor. I asked Kevin what it was. "Rainwater," he said.

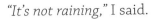

"*It's not raining,*" I said.

"Probably condensation."

"*That much?*" He stuck his finger in it and admitted that the smell couldn't be anything but fuel. He went up to talk to the pilot and immediately the plane started swerving and diving lower. Kevin then announced to us that the pilot knew of a bush strip in the jungle and planned to make a landing. The man behind me said, "Yes, an *emergency* landing." We swerved and dove with fuel in the airplane, more coming in all of the time. Believe me, it was quite nerve-wracking, especially when I got a glimpse of the postage-stamp size of bush strip carved from the jungle. One little spark while landing? I didn't want to think about it.

Thank goodness we landed safely. All of us immediately got out so that we wouldn't be in the plane with the fuel. It was quiet all around us in knee-high grass. Suddenly people started streaming out of the jungle with their machetes, bush knives, and axes. It made me think of the gruesome scars I had witnessed at the resort. We started acting like ambassadors, smiling, shaking hands, and going from person to person all of whom seemed curious to know why we were there. Eventually, as I got farther from the plane, I found a woman dressed in blue. She could speak English, and I asked her if she had a job here. She said that she worked in a hospital. I asked if she had many patients. She said not many now, but recently they'd had a lot because of *clan wars*. In fact, she said that everyone was very excited to see an airplane, because that bush strip hadn't been landed on for *eight months* due to clan wars. Yikes! Not long after that someone told me to get back to the plane immediately. By that time we were surrounded by a crush of about 300 people (with their weapons). The pilot wanted us back on the plane, but two of the natives had their arms across the steps and wouldn't let us get back on! Although most of the people were friendly, there started to be shouting at the men who wouldn't let us on. Then another couple of men started physically tussling with them. That's when Garland started getting nervous. We didn't want there to be a physical disagreement, perhaps starting another clan war, with us in the middle of it.

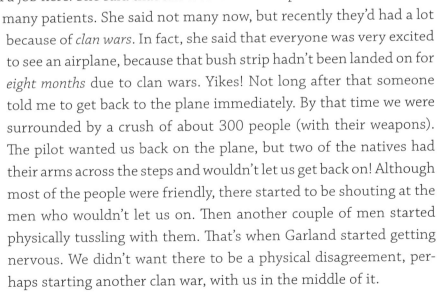

Thankfully this was near a Baptist mission, which explained the hospital. The native pastor showed up to try to mediate. Meanwhile, more teenager types were running towards us with axes. One of

Adventure & Appliqué ❦ Suzanne Marshall

the passengers later admitted he thought they meant to ax the plane's tires. Our guide got smart. He found a piece of paper and made a very official looking "document" to give to the men with the name of the plane, the numbers on it, and their names so that they could make an "official" complaint, in case it was money they were after.

Finally, we were able to get back on the plane, though we still had to try to take off on that tiny strip. Meanwhile, fuel sloshed around the plane with more coming in! This time, we flew at a height skimming the tops of the trees rather than cruising high in the air. I kept wondering if it was so that we would be closer to the ground in case we crashed. I couldn't think about anything else because my lungs were burning from the smell. I really thought I would probably die! After half an hour we came to the field where we were supposed to land. It was flooded!

Never mind. We found another field ten minutes later where we safely landed. Two days later, we had to get back on the same plane. By then they had fixed the fuel leak. Thank goodness! I lay in bed that night pinching myself, surprised to still be alive.

How thankful I was to have a quilt on the trip to work on, helping me focus on the embroidery instead of wondering if our plane would crash in the jungle.

SEWING TIP

Always take a quilt along on a trip. You never know when you might be stuck in an airport or need some distraction after a harrowing experience. ❧

THE BEAST AND HIS BOY
56" x 43" ✦ 2007

THE BEAST AND HIS BOY was inspired by tapestries woven in Basel, Switzerland (ca 1430–1440). Many of these fifteenth-century upper Rhine tapestries were religious in nature and used in churches. The weavings popular for private use often contained elegantly dressed young men and women leading huge fantastic beasts. These implied moral or allegorical messages. They were used as wallhangings for both decoration and insulation.

The judges speak their minds ...

This quilt won the Best Use of Thread award at the 2007 Quilters' Heritage Celebration in Lancaster, Pennsylvania.

- 👑 This is a fabulous piece! The attention to detail brings the viewer in and the fine workmanship keeps them there.
- 👑 Clearly, much thought has gone into each element. Great expressions on the characters.
- 👑 Ombre background a great choice, and you had the forethought to put the dark at the top.
- 👑 Successful handling of a design that could have seemed too crowded, but your stitched detailing takes care of this.
- 👑 A good strong design.

The basilisk (a legendary dragon with lethal breath and glance) stood for envy. The sprays of flowers held by the man were intended to quiet the beast by their scent. The birds were meant to represent a presence symbolically opposite that of the beast, an allegorical reminder of the power of good and evil (Donald King, issue 53, October 1990, *HALI* magazine, pp. 144–153).

Garland shares his thoughts...

Not only are the "zahm und wild" (calm and wild) tapestries of the upper Rhine exceptional folk art, but only a relative few (135) are know to have survived. One (only 3'1" x 6'5") which once hung in the Benedictine Abbey of Muri in Canton Aargau, Switzerland, sold at Christie's in 1990 for over one million dollars to the Canton Aargau Historisches Museum. An excellent reference on these tapestries is Zahm und Wild *by Anna Rapi Buri and Monica Stucky-Schurer, published by Verlag Philipp von Zabern of Mainz am Rhein, Germany in 1990. It helps to read German, but the illustrations are superb even if you don't. The best reference we have found in English is the article In HALI by Donald King.* ⚜

1170 (Eleven Seventy) • 40" x 55" • 2007

Adventure & Appliqué ← Suzanne Marshall

1170 (ELEVEN SEVENTY) ◆ 40" x 55" ◆ 2007

ELEVEN SEVENTY was adapted from part of the Stammheim Missal, which was created in and for the north German monastery of Saint Michael at Hildesheim. It includes David and companion musicians.

The judges speak their minds ...

- There are areas that have stretched, causing puffiness
- Excellent use of color; fabrics chosen are harmonious yet high in contrast
- Border and binding are subtly colored to highlight the central design motifs
- Outstanding use of embroidery techniques
- Stitches are even and lie flat
- Complex yet integrated design
- Corners nicely mitered
- Stunning; appliqué and embroidery nicely done ✾

Sharing What I've Learned

I can't believe what fun I've had teaching hand appliqué and hand quilting around the country, as well as in Africa, Australia, and Europe. I've come to the conclusion that quilters across the globe are the best folks to be with. During my travels, I have found quilters on the whole to be wholesome, motivated, eager to learn, interested in other people, giving, friendly, and very talented.

Garland shares his thoughts ...

One of the real joys of occasionally accompanying Suzanne on her many trips to lecture and teach are the people I get to meet. Quilters are real people like those I grew up with, seldom overwhelmed with their own self-importance. During one trip, I learned more about the sex life and its impact on hunting turkeys than I thought existed. I also enjoy "show and tell" where I get to see just how creative and innovative today's quilters have become.

I love my students. It's sad to part from them after a great class. They often ask me questions, which I try to answer. They also tell me "funnies" which I love!

The best "funny" was told to me by one of my local St. Louis students. After finishing her food, my student would appliqué for the remainder of lunch while she visited with her male coworkers who usually played cards. One day the guys asked my student what she was making. She held her sewing up high to show them, and she had sewed it to her skirt! Every day after that, the guys asked her, *"What are you making?!?!"*

Now here's another story told to me by one of my students. Unfortunately, it's not really a "funny."

My student's quilt guild spent months making a beautiful raffle quilt. It was a truly lovely design with intricate hand stitching. They sold many tickets, and the winner was a young woman who was absolutely thrilled when guild members brought the quilt to her home. As they presented the quilt to her, she said, "I just *love* wrapping a quilt around myself so tightly I can hear the stitches pop!"

When I start teaching a class, I have to admit to my students that I've never taken one! I've learned the hard way—by trial and error. But because of that, I have developed some new methods on my own.

I usually tell my class that what I have to teach is what has worked for me. I don't know all of the many ways to do things, but I can share what I do and hope that it helps them. If it does, *great!* If not, then I ask that they keep exploring and find their own way.

I truly believe that everyone has to find what works for *them* and then just do it. No one knows after a quilt is finished what thread was used, what needle was used, whether it was needle-turned or freezer-papered. Yes, it's pretty obvious whether it was machine or hand quilted, but for the hand quilting, who can tell whether it was in a frame or a hoop or just lap quilted? If the quilt satisfies the maker, that's the important thing.

As you see, I have included judges' comment on my quilts throughout this book. It's not hard to notice that even judges don't always agree and that's as it should be. Everyone has personal tastes and there is no such thing as a universally perfect quilt. Good workmanship always shows and creativity always shines, but it is most important to make a quilt that pleases your personal tastes, standards, and vision. You may notice on page 16, one judge comments on my quilt ADORATION OF THE MAGI, "balance of design needs improvements," which gave me a little chuckle. The criticism is very reasonable; however, my goal on that project was to make a quilt that looked crooked yet had perfectly straight edges. Because I was following a historical model and my goals were clear, I feel this quilt is very successful.

Garland shares his thoughts ...

One downside of doing lectures and workshops is the loss of continuity due to new officers at the guilds. One person will request details about Suzanne's workshops/lectures; the job is passed on to another who handles the contract (often a year or two in advance): and a third will host the visit. Yes, Virginia, some details do fall through the cracks. On one recent trip, Suzanne was asked if she really needed a slide projector for her two slide lectures.

Taking the Mystique out of Appliqué

This book is my opportunity to share the knowledge I've acquired and hopefully get some ideas buzzing around in your head. While it's not quite the same as a class, we can still kick some ideas around. There are some questions that seem to get asked time and time again—perhaps you have found yourself wondering about the same things. Let's start with our favorite subject of hand appliqué:

What needle do you like to use?

My favorite needle is a size 10 quilting needle that is stainless steel and made in England. They are distributed by Jean S. Lyle in Quincy, Illinois, and come in a little wooden case. They have an eye large enough to thread even with my bad eyesight and slide easily through fabric. The needle being short, it's easier to make tiny stitches, and since I also use this needle for quilting, I don't have to adjust to a different size for appliqué.

What thread do you like?

Can you believe that I love Coats and Clark Dual Duty Plus® thread? I like cotton thread next to the cotton fabric, but I also like the strength of the polyester core. It is easy to thread in my needle and usually doesn't tangle up or break. One of my students recommended a 60-weight cotton European thread that she loved. I tried it and liked it, too. It melted beautifully into the cotton fabric, but when I was on a trip adding embroidery next to my appliqué, I was horrified to find that some of the threads had broken. I realized that the thread wasn't strong enough for me—maybe I drag my quilts around too much, or maybe it's simply just not strong enough. I'll not use it again and will go back to my Coats and Clark.

Some of my students love silk. Fine. I just find it more difficult to work with. Again, find what works for *you* and keep going.

How do you begin an appliqué piece?

Make a knot in your thread, then come up under the line that marks your seam allowance and hide the knot inside the fold as you begin the appliqué on a piece. Coming up under the background will leave a "tail" that may show through a light fabric if the thread is dark. Play it safe and just get in the habit of hiding the tail inside the fold of the appliqué piece.

How do you end a thread on an appliqué piece?

Take your needle to the back. Make a knot in the background behind the appliqué. Then hide the tail next to the edge of the appliqué before cutting it off.

Do you cut the background out behind an appliqué piece?

Now there's a controversial question! There are many famous quilters who highly recommend leaving the background intact. Then there are others, like *me*, who love cutting out the background.

Reasons given for leaving the background intact:
  - ✦ An unpleasant sunken appearance given to the appliqué
  - ✦ Appliqué may come apart from the background, leaving a hole
  - ✦ Structural integrity compromised
  - ✦ Appliqué shape sinks into the batting, losing the dimensional effect
  - ✦ Underlying fabric gives stability to the quilt top

Reasons given for cutting out the background:
  - ✦ Batting comes up and fills the appliqué, giving it more loft and dimension
  - ✦ Two or more layers of fabric weigh the batting down
  - ✦ One layer of fabric gives a uniform density to the quilt
  - ✦ Eliminates shadowing
  - ✦ Easier hand quilting

Fascinating! The "con" says "an unpleasant sunken appearance." The "pro" says, "batting fills the appliqué and gives more dimension." That is a total contradiction!

To my way of thinking, if a *cotton batting* is used and the background is cut out from behind the appliqué piece, the appliqué will sink into the cotton batting and cling to the cotton, causing a sunken appearance.

If polyester *batting with loft* is used and the background is cut out from behind the appliqué piece, the batting will come up and fill the appliqué, giving more dimension.

Because I use a polyester batting (Hobbs Polydown® batting is my favorite), and because I cut out behind my appliqué, there is a lot of dimension within my pieces. The more the background is quilted, the more the appliqué tends to rise up from it—with the polyester filling the appliqué piece since the background has been cut out. Many people have asked me if my appliqué is *stuffed*, and I have to say no! That's just the polyester filling the appliqué since the background is gone and not inhibiting it. And quilting within the appliqué piece adds even more dimension and gives stability to the piece with less chance of the appliqué pulling away from the background that is left.

I can also quilt inside the appliqué pieces without stress, since there aren't extra layers to quilt through. I do, however, leave the background behind the appliqué pieces that I don't intend to quilt. The seam allowance alone helps give dimension to the very small pieces.

In fact, for many of my multi-pieced appliqués, there is *no background behind the stitching* within the appliqué. Here's how that's done:

1. Appliqué the piece, leaving a ¼"–½" seam allowance that will be left unturned at the place where another appliqué piece will be joined to it.

2. Baste at the very edge of the seam allowance.

3. Cut out behind the appliqué piece down to the basting.

4. Add the next appliqué piece. There is now no background behind the place where the appliqué has been added.

When a multi-pieced pattern is finished, there is no background behind the entire appliqué! How easy is that to quilt.

But hold on a minute now! There's something else that might make all of this work. I ALWAYS MATCH THE GRAIN LINES OF THE APPLIQUÉ PIECE WITH THE GRAIN LINES IN THE BACKGROUND. That gives stability to the piece and prevents the appliqué piece from warping.

Think about it! If you're stitching on the bias part of an appliqué piece and the background happens to be on the straight grain at that point, the appliqué is stretching and the background isn't! Or, if you're stitching on the straight grain of the appliqué piece and it happens to be on the bias part of the background, then the background is stretching away from the appliqué piece. Wouldn't it be better for everything to be *moving or not moving* at the same place at the same time?

Keeping the grain lines matching between the appliqué and the background helps with stability and keeps everything from stretching out of place after the background is cut away. And by using notebook paper for the appliqué templates, it's easy to match the grain lines because of the lines on the notebook paper. See pages 101–104, The Nuts & Bolts of Take-away Appliqué, for step-by-step pictures of the process.

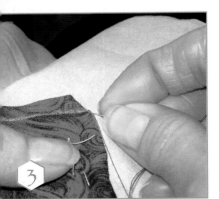
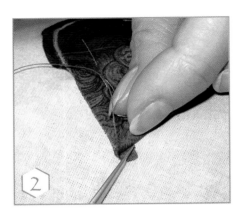
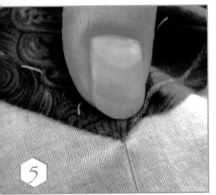

How do you make sharp points?

1. Stitch to the exact place where you want the point to be.

2. Turn the top fabric back and trim the seam allowance underneath on a diagonal. Even trimming a couple of threads will help eliminate bulk.

3. Turn the fabric under straight back at the point and hold it down with your thumb.

4. Turn the fabric under beyond the point—think about pushing it "downhill" from the point.

5. Pull on the thread to extend the point and stitch.

How do you make smooth inside curves?

1. Stop stitching *at least* ¼" to ½" *before* the inside curve.

2. Turn the seam allowance under¼" to ½" *after* the inside curve and hold it down with your thumb.

3. Sweep the needle between your thumb and the last appliqué stitch, smoothly turning under the fabric. In order to do this, lay the needle *flat* across the seam allowance with the point of the needle away from you; then stand the needle up so that the needle pushes towards *you* with the needle appearing in a vertical position.

4. Hold the turned under fabric down with your thumb and stitch.

Is it okay to pin the appliqué pieces to the background before stitching them down?

I really like basting the pieces in place instead of using pins. Since I often take appliqué on trips to work on, I don't risk the chance of dribbling pins all over the place, especially in the doctor's office or in an airplane. I also don't like pricking myself since it might cause me to bleed on my quilt. My threads catch on the pins, too. Besides, pieces appliquéd with pins have much less stability.

Why are my appliqué stitches sometimes visible on the front of the quilt?

First, be sure you are using thread that matches the color of fabric you are appliquéing. Sometimes the appliqué stitches need to be tightened a bit. To see if they are loose, pull on them with your needle on the wrong side of the background fabric. Check the front to see if this helped the visible threads disappear. If it did, try to make your appliqué stitches a bit tighter.

It's possible that a slanted stitch was made on the front, like a whipping stitch. The needle needs to go into the background *right next* to the place where the thread comes out of the appliqué. If the needle is moved forward before going into the background rather than directly next to where the thread comes out, a slanted stitch will be made that will more likely show on the front.

Stitches are more likely to be visible on tightly woven fabrics, such as batiks or those that are hand painted. Keep this in mind during fabric selection and just accept that if batiks are chosen, the stitches won't sink into the cotton as easily as other commercial fabrics.

Tiny stitches also help. Because the needle only moves forward ¹⁄₁₆" to ⅛" underneath the background fabric, when it comes up it catches only a thread or two on the edge of the folded seam allowance of the appliqué before going back into the background right next to that spot.

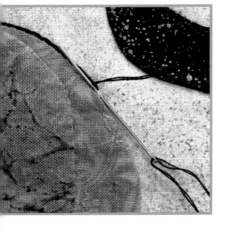

When do you add embroidery to your appliqué? What stitch do you use?

Outline stitch embroidery is added after the appliqué is finished but before the batt and backing have been added. The stitch is made through the background right next to the appliqué with the "ridge" of the stitch on the outside of the appliqué. If another color is added, make the outline stitch right next to the first line of embroidery. It makes an incredible amount of difference to add embroidery.

Look at the two birds and see that one has been outlined with embroidery and the other one has not.

How do you make bias stems for appliqué?

There is an easy way to make bias without needing to purchase a gadget to do so:

1. Cut your fabric in half on the bias.

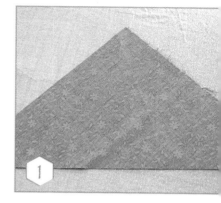

2. Press under a ¼" turn-under allowance on the bias edge of the cloth. This is very easy to do because the fabric is being stabilized by being on the whole cloth. If it were cut in a strip, it would stretch while pressing and would be very easy to burn fingers working with such a narrow piece of fabric.

3. Make another fold that defines the *width* of the bias strip that you want. Press again.

4. Baste down the middle, catching all three layers with your basting stitches. If you have lots of bias to make, you may go to the sewing machine, change the stitch to *baste*, and sew. It helps to loosen the stitches so that they can be more easily pulled out after the appliqué is finished.

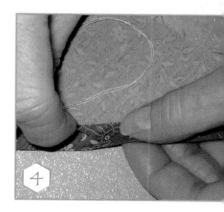

5. Turn the folded fabric back and cut it close to the basting stitches on the underside of the bias strip.

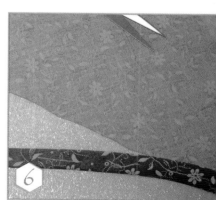

6. Now you have a piece of perfectly basted bias that can be manipulated any way that you want in your appliqué project.

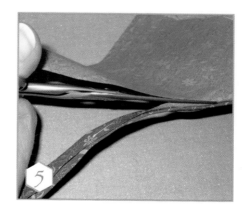

Where do you find your ideas for quilts?

Ideas for quilts can be just about anywhere. Architectural details, ancient embroideries, old tiles, manhole covers, stained-glass windows, vacation photos, and pictures of vintage textiles are just a few examples of things that can be inspiration for quilts. Sometimes just a portion of a picture can inspire the design for an entire quilt.

Explore collections in public libraries as well as museum libraries. University libraries are also valuable for discovering new ideas. I once spent a day in a university library tracking down fabulous designs from nineteenth-century bookbindings. Who knows when that particular quilt will be born?

What do you do if you find a copyright-free picture that you want to adapt to a quilt?

I usually take the picture to a copy machine and enlarge it to the size that I think would be appropriate for a quilt block, wallhanging, or portion of a quilt. This means that I need to enlarge the enlargements and then tape the papers together to make the whole.

At the university bookstore in the art department, it is possible to buy 36" wide paper that is sturdy yet can be seen through for tracing. It is sold inexpensively by the foot off of a big roll. I use this paper to trace the enlargements made from the copy machine, redrawing and adjusting the motifs so that I can adapt them to fabric, often changing many design elements.

I feel that it is important to give credit to the original design source when the quilt is on display at an exhibit. ❧

The Nuts & Bolts of
Take-Away Appliqué

So what is take-away appliqué … and what makes it so special?

Take-away appliqué solves the problem of trying to figure out how to appliqué a multi-pieced pattern so that all of the pieces fit perfectly without marking the background fabric or using transparent overlays. It's also an easy way to control the direction of the fabric grain within your appliqué piece.

Have you ever tried to appliqué a multi-pieced pattern on a marked background and not been able to figure out exactly where to sew each part because the seam allowance of the appliqué covered up some of the markings? This problem is eliminated with take-away appliqué.

This technique uses simple lined notebook paper and can be compared to "working a puzzle backwards." As the pieces from the paper pattern are "taken away" during the appliqué process, the fabric appliqué pieces line up perfectly with what is left of the notebook paper.

An example of take-away appliqué is shown with this little turtle:

1. Here's the turtle pattern.

2. Trace the turtle on lined notebook paper, being sure that the lines on the notebook paper go either horizontally or vertically across the turtle.

3. Cut out the paper turtle. Do not cut the pieces apart.

4. Decide which piece should be appliquéd first. Pick a piece that is underneath other pieces. Cut the first piece off of the turtle, leaving the rest of the turtle whole.

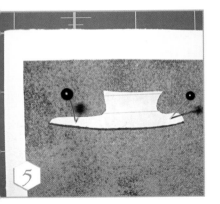

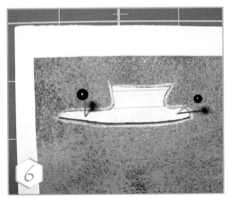

5. Place the fabric right side up on top of a piece of foam board and pin the notebook-paper pattern piece through the fabric and into the foam board in a couple of places to stabilize it, making sure that the lines on the notebook paper are lined up with the grain line on the fabric either vertically or horizontally.

6. Draw around the paper template with a fabric marker. Mark right next to the edge of the paper.

7. Cut out the appliqué piece, adding an approximate ³⁄₁₆" turn-under allowance by eye when cutting. The parts of the piece that will be covered by other appliqué pieces should have at least a ¼" allowance, which will not be turned under. The extra fabric will allow for slight errors in placement.

8. Place the paper turtle on the background in the spot where he will be appliquéd. Slip the fabric appliqué piece under the paper pattern in the gap left by the cut-out piece.

9. Pin the appliqué piece in place and remove the turtle. Baste in place.

10. Appliqué in place and baste with tiny stitches at the edge of the seam allowance that will not be turned under.

11. Cut out behind the appliqué piece. Now there will not be background behind the spot where the next piece will be stitched.

12. Cut off the paper tail, use as a template, and place the fabric tail in the spot where the paper was "taken away."

13. The back leg is next. See how easy it is to place the leg in the exact spot where the paper was "taken away?"

14. Once again, the paper head is used as a template.

15. The rest of the paper turtle shows exactly where the head should be appliquéd.

16. Baste at the very edge of the seam allowance that is not turned under on both the back leg and the head of the turtle.

17. Cut the background out from behind the head and the back leg.

18. After the front leg is appliquéd, the turtle shell fits in place.

19. Appliqué the turtle shell in place.

20. Take the basting stitches out and finish cutting out from behind the turtle.

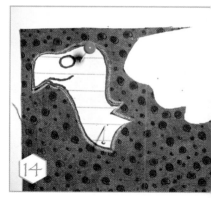

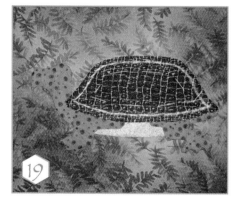

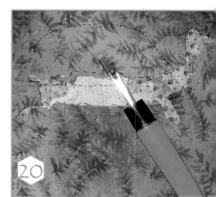

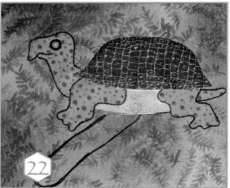

21. Now the turtle has no background from behind the appliqué stitching and will be easy to quilt.

22. Add the eye and embroider around the appliqué pieces on the turtle. ⚜

Quilting on the Go ... Hand Quilting Without a Frame or Hoop

Preparing your quilt for hand quilting.

For hand quilting without a frame or a hoop, there needs to be plenty of basting in the quilt to hold the layers together. Here's what you do:

Pin the backing of the quilt all around the edges to a tightly woven carpet. Use straight pins not safety pins. A shag rug or carpet with long loops won't work. The carpet needs to be similar to an indoor-outdoor or tightly woven Berber type carpet. While pinning the backing, stretch it so that it looks tight. Push the pins through the *edges* of the backing, straight into the carpet and pad under the carpet.

Pat the batting down on the backing, smoothing out any wrinkles. Do not stretch the batting.

Place the top of the quilt on the batting.

Stretch it the same amount that you stretched the backing and pin it through the batting, backing, carpet, and pad all around the edges.

Stand back and look to see that lattice strips or added borders are straight.

At this point the quilt is securely pinned and is held tightly enough to sit in the middle of it to baste. The direction of the basting stitches does not matter. You can make diagonal lines, horizontals, curves, verticals, and circles.

Before lifting the quilt from the carpet, remove the pins and baste in smaller stitches around the edge so that there won't be puckers when the binding is added.

Lift the quilt from the carpet and turn it over. Check to see that it looks firmly basted on the back. You should feel satisfied. It's *highly* unlikely that any wrinkles were basted in.

This is how your quilt should look after the basting is finished. ✤

ABOVE: *A view of the quilt after the basting is finished*

Tips, Tricks &
Other Bits of Experience

Through the years, my students have asked many of the same questions. I've always been delighted to share my recommendations, tips, and tricks with them. Perhaps you've found yourself wondering about some of these things yourself.

What batting do you like to use?

I like to use thin polyester batting because I have better luck making small stitches. I have always used polyester for hand quilting because my needle slides through it easier than with cotton batting, and I want my quilting to be fun—not a struggle. Also, the loft of a polyester batting can fill my appliqué pieces, giving them dimension.

What do you use to mark quilting designs on the quilt top?

For dark fabrics I like to use a Sanford® soft white Prismacolor® pencil. This pencil can be found at art stores or in the art department of university bookstores. The markings show up plainly, and they rub off by the time the quilting is finished. It's always best to experiment first with the pencil you plan to use on the particular fabric in your quilt.

For light fabrics I use a water-soluble pen, taking care to mark lightly so that the mark doesn't go through to the batting. Wipe the marks off with a wet cloth as the quilting is done, and do not expose the marks to heat from either sunshine or an iron. Do not use any detergents on a quilt that has marks from a water-soluble pen. When the quilt is finished, put it in the washing machine in plain water (no soaps) and agitate on the gentle cycle so that the water moving back and forth can take out any residual chemicals from the pen. So far I have not had any trouble with the marks reappearing on my quilts.

How do you make your own templates for quilting designs?

First, find the design that you need in one of the many books, magazines, or sources for quilting patterns. Enlarge or reduce the design to fit the area needed on your quilt. Glue the desired design to cardboard or plastic template material and cut it out.

What tips do you have for making smaller hand quilting stitches?

Use thin polyester batting instead of cotton. Remember that some fabrics are more difficult to stitch through, such as batiks or hand-painted fabrics. I also have occasional difficulty with certain hand-dyed fabrics or white-on-white fabrics.

Pick a backing fabric that is easy to get your needle through. You might ask your local quilt shop owner if you can "audition" a few fabrics in the shop by bringing a small piece of batting and a needle so that you can try the fabric at the edge before purchasing a large piece.

And did you know that you can make smaller stitches by quilting on the bias? Perhaps that's why crosshatching has been so popular throughout the years.

What do you do when your finger gets sore?

I like to use a comfortable thimble on my needle hand. Underneath the quilt where my finger is pricked with the needle, I wrap my finger in electric tape if it gets sore. I can still feel the needle when it comes through the quilt, but the tape helps protect it from the sharp pricks of the needle.

Now that the quilt is basted together. How do I get started?

Because the quilt is not held tightly in a hoop, it can be manipulated to meet your needle. Hold the needle as if you were planning to make a running stitch, stabilizing it with a thimble. Rest your hand holding the needle on your knee or a table—this way there can be a "hoop" of sorts between your two hands. Then with the left hand pinching the quilt underneath, slide the needle through the quilt and prick your finger to be sure that the needle has gone through all of the layers. Bend the quilt backwards, and then lift it up with the finger that was pricked to meet the needle. The quilt actually moves backwards and forwards to meet the needle rather than having the needle "rock" to make the stitches. The thimble stabilizes the needle and pushes while doing this. There is much less stress on the hands quilting this way.

Because the quilt is not being held in a frame or a hoop, it is very easy to turn the quilt in the direction that is easiest for you to make stitches. It is also easy to check the back of the quilt to be sure that the stitches are made evenly.

How do you finish a thread while quilting?

After the last stitch, I usually slip the needle through the batting to a seam line or next to an appliqué piece. I hide a couple of backstitches there. If it is in the middle of background quilting where there isn't a seam or appliqué piece to hide the backstitches, I have the needle travel to another stitch, and I hide a backstitch under that stitch. I then make a knot to pull through in order to hide in the batting. If the needle can travel to an area that will be quilted later, I take a couple of nearly invisible backstitches right on the quilting line to stabilize the thread in that spot. The quilting that goes over this area will go right over the thread and make it impossible to pull out.

You know the old joke about how you get to Carnegie Hall, right? Practice, practice, practice. Good advice for learning to quilt without using a frame or hoop. Practice this style of quilting for 15 minutes a day for six weeks and quilting will become meditative—not a struggle! And the best part is that you'll be able to quilt absolutely ANYWHERE and anytime. ✳

Award-Winning Quilt Patterns

 LEAF HOPPERS, PAGES 110–127

 FIRST RANK, PAGES 128–141

Instructions & Templates for LEAF HOPPERS

1. Cut a piece of graph paper ¼ the size of the desired block.

2. Make a crease mark by folding the graph paper diagonally to allow for a guide when placing the leaf on the block.

3. Place a leaf design in the corner of the graph paper on the diagonal.

4. Place a bug in the middle of the leaf and redraw the legs so that they fit in the leaf.

5. Place a flower, leaf, or another bug at the side of each leaf. Only ½ of the chosen motif needs to be drawn on the graph paper at the sides.

6. Fold a piece of paper in quarters and cut a "snowflake" design to fit under the leaf. Only ¼ of the design is needed for the bottom. When combined with the remaining three quarters, the center of the block will be completed.

7. Make three more copies of the design made on the graph paper.

8. Tape together and start transforming the design to fabric. ❈

Adventure & Appliqué ← Suzanne Marshall

LEAF HOPPERS ✦ *89" x 89"* ✦ *2000*

Adventure & Appliqué ✦ Suzanne Marshall

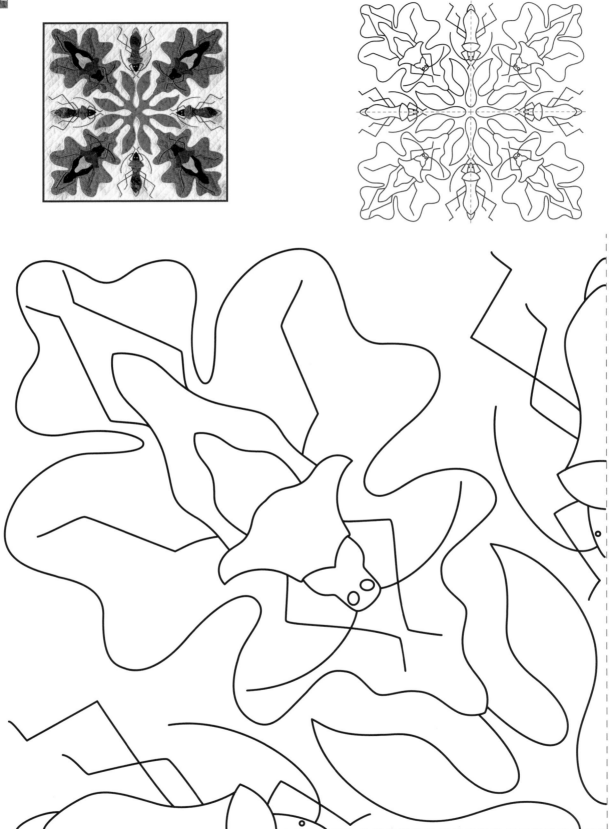

LEAF HOPPERS

Adventure & Appliqué ❧ Suzanne Marshall

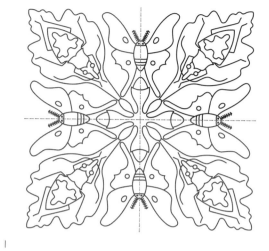

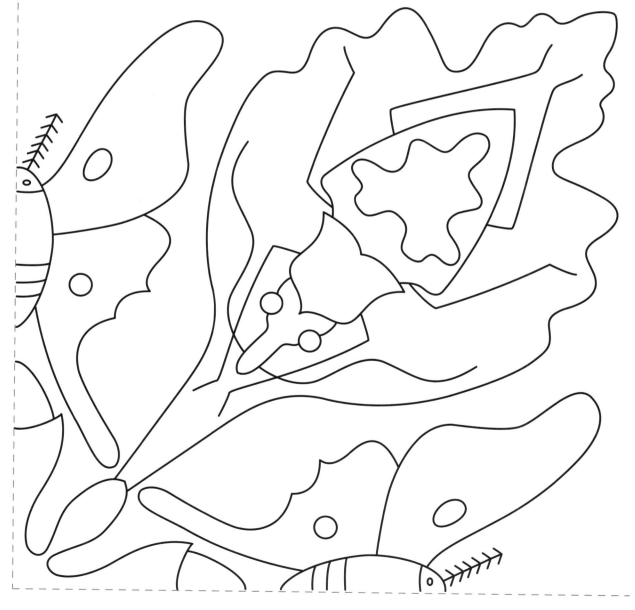

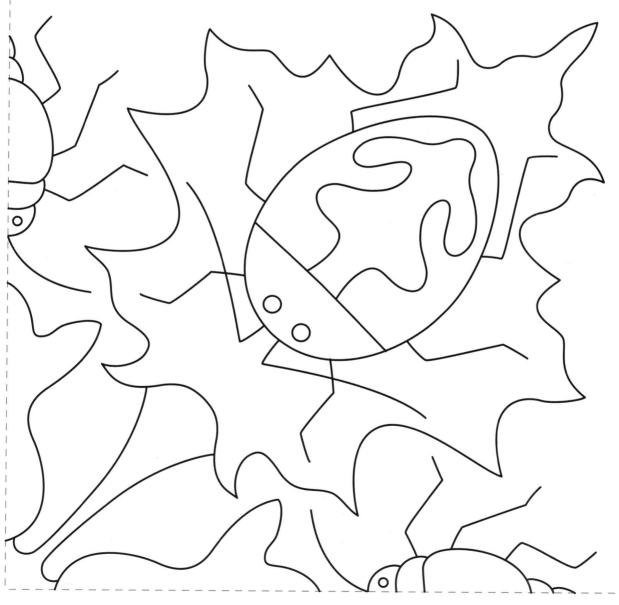

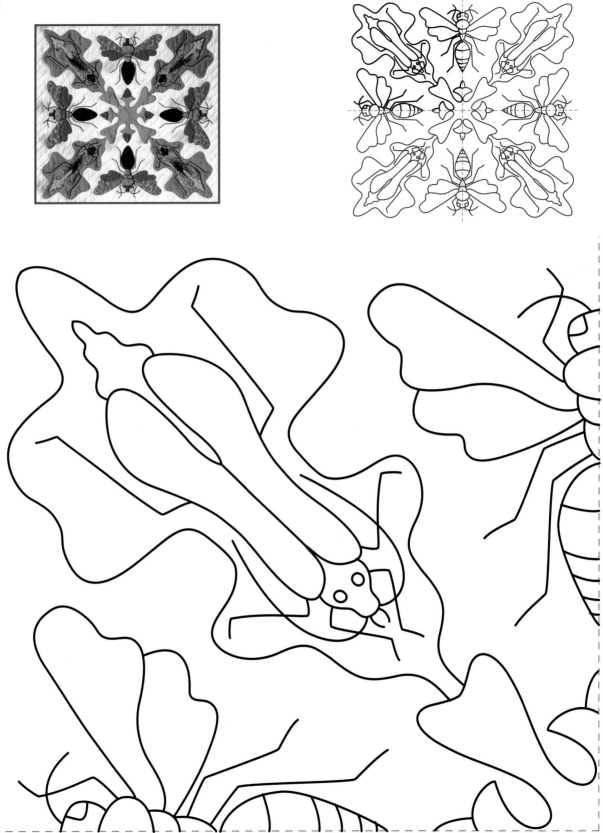

Adventure & Appliqué ✦ Suzanne Marshall

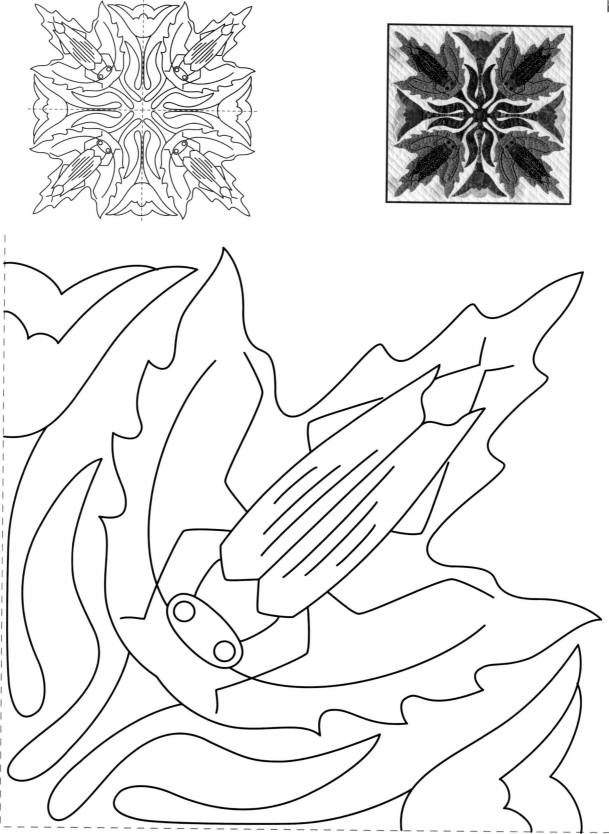

LEAF HOPPERS

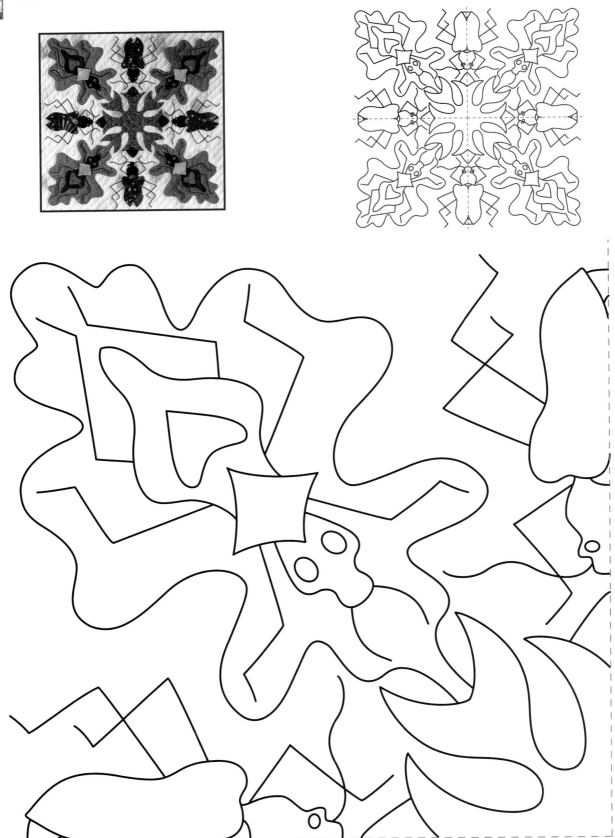

Adventure & Appliqué ← Suzanne Marshall

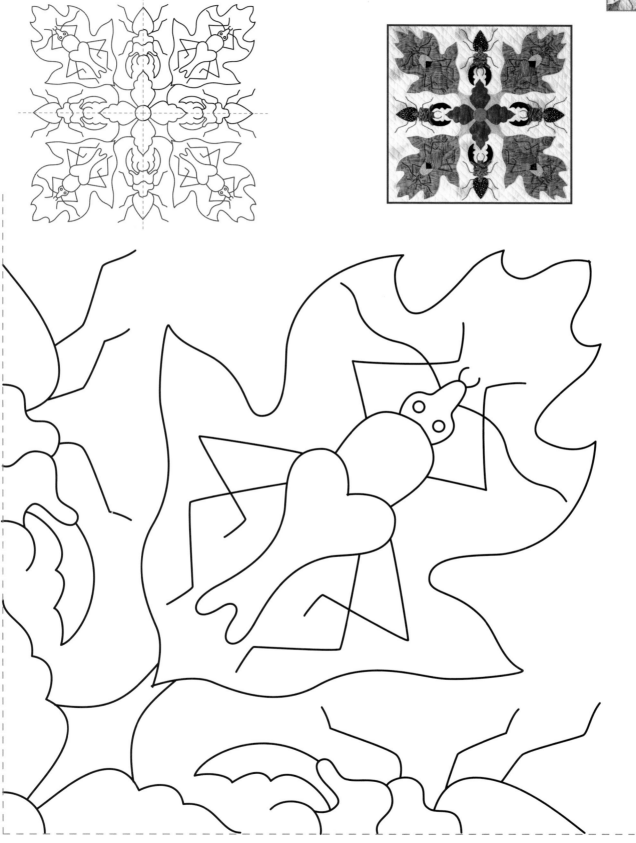

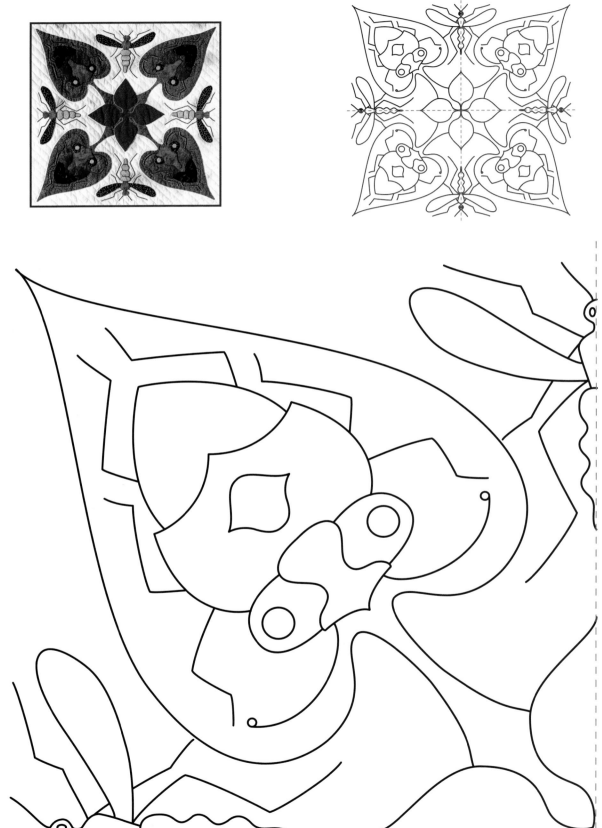

Leaf Hoppers

FIRST RANK ✦ 46" x 46" ✦ 2001

Block placement guide. Individual blocks need to be enlarged 150% for full-size quilt.

1

2

3

5

Adventure & Appliqué ✦ Suzanne Marshall

7

8

9

10

11

12

Shown at 100%

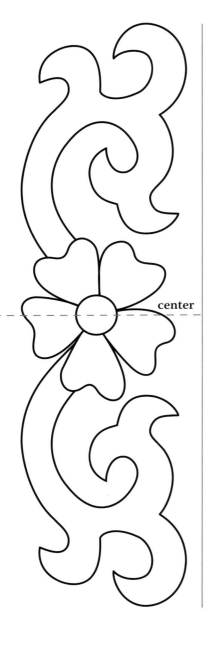

center

center

corner

corner

Adventure & Appliqué ✦ Suzanne Marshall

About the Author
Suzanne Marshall

Award-winning quilter, master appliqué artist, world traveler—these only begin to describe Suzanne Marshall.

Her quilts have been exhibited in museums both here and abroad and have won numerous major awards from too many prestigious quilt shows to mention separately. All this has been accomplished by a self-taught quilter who traces her development to a library book and a collection of fabric scraps, gathered through many years of making clothing.

Inspired by the designs in the textiles of cultures around the world, her quilts reflect her love of both adventure and appliqué.

Born in Joplin, Missouri, Suzanne makes her home in St. Louis with her husband, Garland, where she enjoys visits from her three grown sons and a daughter.

Other AQS Books

This is only a small selection of the books available from the American Quilter's Society. AQS books are known worldwide for timely topics, clear writing, beautiful color photos, and accurate illustrations and patterns. The following books are available from your local bookseller, quilt shop, or public library.

#7602   us$26.95

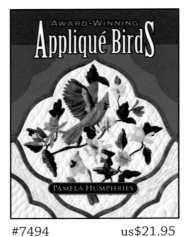

#7494   us$21.95

#7013   us$24.95

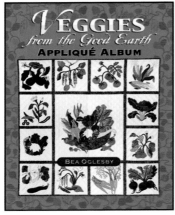

#7017   us$21.95

#7073   us$24.95

#7012   us$19.95

#7010   us$21.95

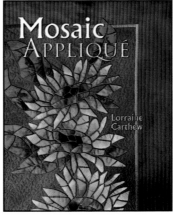

#7071   us$22.95

#7016   us$22.95